NEGLIGENCE
WITHOUT
FAULT

ALBERT A. EHRENZWEIG

Professor of Law, University of California

Berkeley

Trends toward an
Enterprise Liability for Insurable Loss

Negligence
Without
Fault

BERKELEY AND LOS ANGELES

UNIVERSITY OF CALIFORNIA PRESS

1951

UNIVERSITY OF CALIFORNIA PRESS
BERKELEY AND LOS ANGELES, CALIFORNIA

CAMBRIDGE UNIVERSITY PRESS
LONDON, ENGLAND

TO MY FATHER

CONTENTS

Part Two: THE TRUE RULE: "NEGLIGENCE WITHOUT FAULT"

THE NEW RATIONALE

FAULT AND NON-FAULT LIABILITY FOR NEGLIGENCE DISTINGUISHED AND RECONCILED: SUMMARY AND OUTLOOK

§ 1.
INTRODUCTION

Four children chasing a kite drowned in a frozen pond.[1] Damages were sought from a railroad company by whose admitted negligence water had been diverted to form the fatal pond. The Supreme Court of Pennsylvania denied liability because a prudent man in the defendant's place could not have "anticipated and foreseen this unfortunate happening" and because "there was no breach of duty to the children."[2] Jury verdict, majority opinion, and dissent reflect the uncertainty and hesitation prevailing in the allo-

---

[1] But for Professor E. W. Patterson's untiring advice and encouragement, this paper could not have been written. It seeks to establish a theory previously discussed by the writer in an unsigned Note, *Loss-Shifting and Quasi-Negligence: A New Interpretation of the Palsgraf Case*, 8 U. of CHI. L. REV. 729 (1941) (cited as *Loss-Shifting*); in *Soldiers' Liability for Wrongs Committed on Duty*, 30 CORN. L. Q. 179 (1944); and in two Studies prepared for the State of New York Law Revision Commission [Multiple Damages, Leg. Doc. (1944) No. 65 (J), and products Liability, Leg. Doc. (1943) No. 65 (J) (cited as *Products Liability*)]; and further developed in *Assurance Oblige—A Comparative Study*, 15 LAW AND CONTEMP. PROB. 445 (1950) (cited as *Assurance Oblige*) [also Versicherung als Haftungsgrund, 72 JURIST. BLAETTER 253 (Vienna 1950); El Seguro Obliga, 3 BOL. del INST. de DER. COMP. de MEXICO 3 (1950)]. Much I owe to Dean Smith and Professor Llewellyn of the School of Law of Columbia University and to Dean Prosser of the School of Law at the University of California, Berkeley.

[2] Irwin Savings & Trust Co. v. Pa. R. R., 349 Pa. 278, 37 A. (2d) 432 (1944). For a note on cases dealing with similar fact situations, see 10 U. of PITTSBURGH L. REV. 97 (1948). Cf. infra note 62; Part II, notes 40, 143.

cation of the losses caused by the hazards of modern mechanical enterprise.

To create a balance between social and individual interests in this field has been the task and toil of the courts. Every year thousands of accidents foreseeably resulting from hazardous activities, seem to demand full liability to the innocent victim. But the law, for the sake of social gain and progress, has limited that liability to one for a "negligence" measured by "proximate causation" and "duty of care." On the other hand, so greatly have these tests been blunted in their application to enterprise-defendants that their results are "little short of unanimity for the injured party."[3] Jury verdicts are permitted to stand though supported by no more evidence than that of some kind of formal fault; plaintiffs are assisted by fictions and presumptions (§ 4); and liability insurance, devised for the injurer's protection, has widely been adapted to secure the recovery of the injured (§§ 6, 11). The Supreme Court itself, having greatly extended the negligence liability of "Federal Employers" (§ 4), has been accused by a dissenting Justice of leaving the fault principle without much practical meaning.[4] A new law of enterprise liability is in the making. To analyze this process in legal history, present theory and future probabilities both in legislative and judicial law making, is the purpose of this study.

The term "negligence" implies blame for "neglect." The attempt will be made to show how and why the courts have come to make this concept with its inherent *censure* (§§ 2, 17)

[3] GREEN, JUDGE AND JURY 139 (1930). For references to recent statistics see James, *Functions of Judge and Jury in Negligence Cases*, 58 YALE L. J. 667, 687 (1949). See also Prosser, *Proximate Cause in California*, 38 CALIF. L. REV. 369, 397 (1950); McCord, *Are You Your Brother's Keeper?* [1950] INS. L. J. 709 (1950).

[4] Jackson, J., in Wilkerson v. McCarthy, 336 U.S. 53, 76, 69 Sup. Ct. 413, 424 (1949), where a railroad was held liable for negligence to a switchman who had fallen into defendant's pit though posts and chains had been erected to prevent employees from entering the area. See also O'Donnell v. Elgin, J. & E. R.R., 338 U.S. 384, 70 Sup. Ct. 200 (1949); Affolder v. New York, C. & St. L. R.R., 339 U.S. 96, 70 Sup. Ct. 509 (1950) (liability under Federal Safety Appliances Act).

the basis and measure of *compensation* for harm caused by *lawful* activities (§§ 3-8); and what this has done to the concept and law of negligence (§§ 9-11). A negligence verdict condemning the substandard conduct of a drunken driver does not mean the same thing as a negligence verdict distributing losses caused by the lawful operation of a railroad corporation (§ 12). The resulting equivocations in the negligence rule may often have proved valuable in promoting sound compromise between competing policies. But if these equivocations are to continue as a vehicle of progress, they must be analyzed and recognized as such lest they hamper the organic growth of the law (§§ 12-17).

Many crosscurrents and transitions make impossible an exhaustive classification of the liabilities now included in the "negligence" rule. But certain groups of those liabilities, being clearly related to "strict" liabilities (§§ 13-15), permit and indeed require a separate analysis and nomenclature. These groups of liabilities, after a brief discussion of their history and present crisis (§§ 5-8), will be analyzed as quasi-strict liabilities for *"negligence without fault"* (§ 16). Elsewhere I suggested that this type of negligence be termed "quasi-negligence,"[5] as the basis of a non-fault liability within the framework of the traditional language of negligence. However, this terminology has been abandoned in this study to take account of the fact that we have come to think of this "quasi-negligence" as of the negligence of our daily lives distinguishing therefrom as "gross," "wanton," or "wilful" negligence most of what remains of the original "moral" concept (§ 23).

---

[5] *Loss-Shifting,* supra note 1, 736 n.38. This term abbreviates the awkward though more accurate phrase "quasi-strict liability for quasi-negligence." Cf. the use of the terms "quasi-tort" in Wu, *Two Forms of Tortious Liability in the Modern Chinese Law,* THE ART OF LAW 70 (1936); and "legal fault" in F. F. Stone, *Touchstones of Tort Liability,* 2 STAN. L. REV. 259, 283 (1950). Professor James approves the phrase "negligence without fault." James, *Statutory Standards and Negligence in Accident Cases,* 11 LA. L. REV. 95 (1950). For an earlier related analysis see Vold, *The Functional Perspective for the Law of Torts,* 14 NEB. L. BULL. 217, 236 (1936).

Before the negligence rule ("the rule invoked"), as applied to enterprise liability, can be restated in terms of a new "true" rule of "negligence without fault," that rule must be proved to be the "better rule" as to simplicity, clarity, and compatibility, as well as the "real rule" appearing in the "actual doing" of the courts.[6] Thus, the new rule will have to be tested as to damages, conflict of laws, pleading and jury practice; as to the several types of tortfeasors (including employer and employee, automobile owner and operator, manufacturer and retailer, trustee and trust estate, government and official); and as to the several torts (including nuisance, deceit, libel, and breach of warranty). A brief outline of some results expected from such an investigation will be given at this time (§§ 17-23).

Enterprise liability for negligence without fault has been promoted by, and has in turn promoted, the institution of liability insurance as a means of the injured's compensation. I attempted elsewhere to follow this development through several foreign legal systems.[7] The next logical step in the protection of persons injured by hazardous activities would be the adoption of schemes of compulsory liability insurance.[8] The opposition to such schemes is partly caused, I believe, by the failure to segregate consciously an enterprise liability whose limits could be determined by its very insurability. It can only be a matter of conjecture, whether developments such as the "medical first payment revolution," which would secure certain benefits of automobile "liability insurance" to passengers and bystanders without regard to liability,[9] or the "liability" insurance of immune

---

[6] See Llewellyn, *On Reading and Using the Newer Jurisprudence*, 40 COL. L. REV. 581, 608 (1940).

[7] *Assurance Oblige*, supra note 1.

[8] See e.g., Grad, *Recent Developments in Automobile Accident Compensation*, 50 COL. L. REV. 300 (1950); *Assurance Oblige*, supra note 1, at 449; Note, *Saskatchewan Automobile Accident Insurance Act* [1950] INS. L.J. 702 (1950); SHAWCROSS, THE LAW OF MOTOR INSURANCE (2d ed. 1949) 379; infra note 158.

[9] See Yore, *Automobile Medical Payments Coverage Points a New Way*, SPECTATOR, Feb. 22, 1940. "First Aid Clauses" cover expenses for immediate surgical and medical aid to any third party, while so-called

tortfeasors (§§ 6, 21), will initiate a semisocial *"third party beneficiary insurance"* which would distribute losses caused by hazardous enterprise without regard to the entrepreneur's liability.

The peculiarity of the present project which, to discover and promote trends, must presuppose much that might still be subject to controversy, may justify a somewhat unorthodox technique. In stating settled doctrine references to textbooks and law review articles have seemed more appropriate than citations of cases arbitrarily chosen from boundless accumulations. Living law is shown as it appears from encyclopedic case summaries and "business" literature, in a field in which case law has become so redundant that surveys of fact situations catering to the practitioner's needs have largely replaced the analysis of judicial opinion. Where, however, growing or future law is investigated, such analysis is indispensable to show characteristic divergences between rules avowedly and actually followed. For this purpose, to illustrate trends, views expressed in dissents, minority jurisdictions, and obiter dicta are as valuable as, or more valuable than, majority opinions purportedly following traditional doctrines. Similar considerations may justify the liberal use of quotations where language is our best guide to thought.

"medical indorsements" entitle occupants of the insured's car to medical expenses within specified limits. 8 APPLEMAN, INSURANCE LAW AND PRACTICE §§ 4895, 4896 (1942, Supp. 1949). This type of insurance seems to be spreading both to new types of accidents and new groups of persons. See 48 BEST'S No. 2, 45 (1947); *Spectator*, Feb. 14, 1946; James, *Accident Liability Reconsidered: The Impact of Liability Insurance*, 57 YALE L.J. 565 (1948); James and Thornton, *The Impact of Insurance on the Law of Torts*, 15 LAW AND CONTEMP. PROB. 431 (1950).

Part One

THE RULE INVOKED: "NEGLIGENCE"

"'The rule is settled,' the Sirens sung."

Llewellyn, *Put in His Thumb* 45 (1931)

THE GROWTH OF THE RULE

§ 2.   I. PREINDUSTRIAL PERIOD

The history of tort law is determined by the search for a compromise between an "injurer's" law based on the injurer's conduct[10] and an "injured's"[11] law satisfying the injured.[12] Since the oldest tort law of vengeance implied blame,[13] it punished fault; but it also protected the injured since it presumed fault even in the "misdeeds" of inanimate things.[14] The injured's interests continued to prevail even

[10] See Morris, *Punitive Damages in Tort Cases*, 44 HARV. L. REV. 1173 (1931); Cooley, *Problems in Contributory Negligence*, 89 U. OF PA. L. REV. 335, 338 n.12 (1940). See in general PROSSER, HANDBOOK OF THE LAW OF TORTS (hereinafter referred to as TORTS) 27 (1941).

[11] These helpful terms, though not in general use, are listed in 5 MURRAY, A NEW ENGLISH DICTIONARY ON HISTORICAL PRINCIPLES 301 (1901).

[12] See e.g. Radin, *A Speculative Inquiry into the Nature of Torts*, 21 TEX. L. REV. 697, 703 (1943); 1 STREET, THE FOUNDATIONS OF LEGAL LIABILITY 477 (1906); Jenks, *Theories of Tort in Modern Law*, 19 L. Q. REV. 19 (1903); Takayanagi, *Liability without Fault in the Modern Civil and Common Law*, 16 ILL. L. REV. 163, 268; 17 ILL. L. REV. 187, 416 (1921-1923); James, *Accident Liability: Some Wartime Developments*, 55 YALE L. J. 365, 366 (1946); LAWSON, NEGLIGENCE IN THE CIVIL LAW (Oxford, 1950).

[13] See HOLMES, THE COMMON LAW 10 et seq. (1881). This psychological interpretation of absolute liability as a liability for "fault" could perhaps reconcile the seemingly inconsistent "absolute liability" theories [Wigmore, *Responsibility for Tortious Acts: Its History*, 3 SELECT ESSAYS IN ANGLO-AMERICAN LEGAL HISTORY 475 et seq. (1909), revised and brought up to date from 7 HARV. L. REV. 315, 383, 442 (1894)] and "fault" theories [Winfield, *The Myth of Absolute Liability*, 42 L. Q. REV. 37 (1926)] on the origin of tort law. See also Thayer, *Liability without Fault*, 29 HARV. L. REV. 810 (1916).

[14] See *Loss-Shifting*, op. cit. supra note 1, 735 n.33; HOLMES, op.

when government sanction had replaced the feud,[15] and even when refined psychological reflection and the powerful moral philosophy of the Church had brought increased protection for the injurer by first making rebuttable and then abolishing the presumption of fault.[16] The law of civil liability did "not so much regard the intent of the actor, as the loss and the damage of the party suffering."[17]

True, at the end of the nineteenth century compromise seemed to have yielded to a general dogma of "no liability without fault."[18] However, the idea of compensation for the injured, with little or no regard for the injurer's fault, had been preserved in many special rules such as those concerning trespass to land and conversion, or liabilities for animals and dangerous things and of insane persons;[19] and instances

cit. supra note 13, at 11. For a history of the "deodand," the noxal surrender of "guilty" things, see id. at 7 et seq.

[15] See Woodbine, *The Origin of the Action of Trespass*, 33 YALE L. J. 799 (1924); 34 YALE L. J. 343 (1925); Wigmore, op. cit. supra note 13, 504; PROSSER, TORTS 37, 77, 94; STREET, op. cit. supra note 12, 77. See in general 1 SIMPSON AND STONE, LAW AND SOCIETY, Part I, chap. iv; Part II, chap. iii.

[16] See Weaver v. Ward, Hob. 134, 80 Eng. Rep. 284 (1616). In criminal law the king's pardon brought relief in certain typical situations of "misadventure." See Moreland, *A Rationale of Criminal Negligence*, 32 KY. L. J. 1, 127, 221, 3 n.6 (1943-1944). For a history of the fault requirement since Brown v. Kendall, 6 Cush. 292, 60 Mass. 292 (1850) see Wigmore, op. cit. supra note 13, 503 ff.

[17] Lambert & Olliot v. Bessey, T. Raym, 421, 422 (K. B. 1681).

[18] See Ames, *Law and Morale*, 22 HARV. L. REV. 97, 99 (1908) ("The ethical standard of reasonable conduct has replaced the immoral standard of acting at one's peril"); Morris, *Punitive Damages in Tort Cases*, 44 HARV. L. REV. 1173 (1931); HOLMES, op. cit. supra note 13, at 144; J. Smith, *Tort and Absolute Liability*, 30 HARV. L. REV. 241, 319, 409 (1917).

[19] Representative cases are: Perry v. Jefferies, 61 S. C. 292, 39 S. E. 515 (1901) (trespass); Hyde v. Noble, 13 N. H. 494, 38 Am. Dec. 508 (1843) (conversion); McKee v. Trisler, 311 Ill. 536, 143 N. E. 69 (1924) and Brackenborough v. Spalding U. D. C., L. R. [1942] A. C. 310 (animals); Rylands v. Fletcher, infra §§ 13, 20 (dangerous things); Davis v. Niagara Falls Tower Co., 171 N. Y. 336, 64 N. E. 4 (1902) (nuisance); Williams v. Hays, 143 N. Y. 442, 38 N. E. 449 (1894), 157 N. Y. 541, 52 N. E. 589 (1899) (insane and infants); Van Vooren v. Cook, 273 App. Div. 88, 75 N. Y. S. (2d) 362 (4th Dept., 1947) (insane). In general see

of such liabilities continued to be added by new interpretations of ancient common law (explosives and blasting, "breach of warranty")[20] as well as by modern legislation (workmen's compensation). Moreover, at the very time the fault dogma seemed to have reached its climax, it had been made to serve the injured's protection in many ways: Although fault was to be a condition of recovery, such fault was again presumed,[21] and causation "spoke for itself."[22] Fault was seen where, innocent as the "wrongdoer" might have been, a "reasonable man" would have acted differently;[23] and under the principle of "respondeat superior" another's fault could be a basis of liability.[24] No wonder then that this law of an "emasculated," "legal," or "objective" fault,[25] though rationalized in a language of "social" morality,[26] soon found a new interpretation.

PROSSER, TORTS 428, 432, 443, 446, 1085, 1089; James, supra note 12, 366 ff.; infra §§ 3, 8, 20.

[20] See Hay v. Cohoes Co., 2 N. Y. 159, 51 Am. Dec. 279 (1849) (blasting); Products Liability, supra note 1, passim; Ultramares Corp. v. Touche, 255 N. Y. 170, 174 N. E. 441 (1931) ("deceit" by accountants' advice); Coffey v. Midland Broadcasting Co., 8 F. Supp. 889 (D. C. W. D. Mo. 1934) (radio defamation).

[21] See J. Smith, Surviving Fictions, 27 YALE L. J. 147 (1917); Bohlen, The Effect of Rebuttable Presumptions of Law upon the Burden of Proof, 68 U. of PA. L. REV. 307 (1920); Harris, Liability without Fault, 6 TULANE L. REV. 337, 338 (1932). For a natural law justification of this presumption see THOMASIUS, FUNDAMENTA JURIS NATURAE ET GENTIUM, I, 10 (1728) who advocates the presumption of fault, "because injuries are frequently inflicted by fault and the law should fit what most frequently happens." For the presumption of fault in modern Continental law see the writer's TORT LIABILITY FOR FAULT (SCHULDHAFTUNG IM SCHADENERSATZRECHT) (Manz, Vienna: 1936) 34, 42, 53, 66, 69, 182, 184, 187, 233.

[22] See infra § 3.

[23] See infra § 9.

[24] See Y. B. Smith, Frolic and Detour, 23 COL. L. REV. 444, 458 (1923); Seavey, Speculations as to "Respondeat Superior," HARVARD LEGAL ESSAYS 433 (1934) and infra § 4.

[25] See infra §§ 9, 17. Seavey, supra note 20, 439 contrasts the "legal fault" of civil liability with the "moral fault" of criminal responsibility. But see Ames, supra note 18.

[26] See RESTATEMENT, TORTS § 282, comment 3 (1934); PROSSER, TORTS 18, 426.

As late as 1898 Lord Herschell considered all legal sanctions as designed to deter.[27] But now the "unreasonable man" is seen as acting "at his peril,"[28] usually without regard to ideas of punishment or deterrence.[29] And Section 519 of the Torts "Restatement" of the American Law Institute would impose liability for the "unpreventable miscarriage" of "ultrahazardous" activities.[30] If this be the trend today, the courts, at least in their language, have failed to concede the change, since the rules of enterprise liability are still couched in terms which imply reprehensible conduct. This fact has, on the one hand, helped to preserve the essentially admonitory institution of punitive damages[31] and, on the other hand, tended to revive the injurer's protection by producing the doctrines of proximate causation, breach of duty, and contributory negligence.[32] The same rationale has given new incentive to the struggle against the liability of the substandard man[33] and of the insane;[34] has encouraged

[27] Allen v. Flood [1898] A.C. 1, 131. Cf. STREET, op. cit. supra note 12, 478 n.4: "This looks very much like an effort to give an appearance of modern refinement to a crude instinct which nevertheless is one of the mainsprings of human action in all stages of society." See also, SALMOND, LAW OF TORTS 13, 18 (10th ed. 1945).

[28] HOLMES, op. cit. supra note 13, 51.

[29] See PROSSER, TORTS 11.

[30] See infra § 14.

[31] See Morris, supra note 18, 1176 et seq.; and the writer's study on "*Multiple Damages,*" supra note 1.

[32] Butterfield v. Forrester (K. B. 1809) 11 East 60, 103 Eng. Rep. 926. This defense was in turn limited in the injured's favor by the doctrines of "last clear chance" [Davies v. Mann (Exch. 1842) 10 M. & W. 546, 152 Eng. Rep. 588], "absolute nuisance" [Beckwith v. Stratford, 129 Conn. 506, 29 A. (2d) 775 (1942)] and "wilful and wanton conduct" [Karanovich v. George, 348 Pa. 199, 34 A. (2d) 523 (1943)].

[33] See Seavey, *Negligence—Subjective or Objective?*, 41 HARV. L. REV. 1 (1927); Moreland, supra note 16, 172; PROSSER, TORTS 224 and cases cited; Note, 8 U. of PITTSBURGH L. REV. 274 (1942) (blind persons). On the converse situation in the expert's liability see e.g., Swan, *The California Law of Malpractice of Physicians, Surgeons, and Dentists*, 33 CALIF. L. REV. 248, 252 (1945).

[34] See, e.g., Williams v. Hays, supra note 19; Hornblower, *Insanity and the Law of Negligence*, 5 COL. L. REV. 278, 284 (1905). For foreign laws see Takayanagi, supra note 12, 16 ILL. L. REV. 299 ff.

the proposals for contribution between tortfeasors;[35] and has caused the recognition of "degrees" of fault and fault liability which probably play a much larger part than is usually supposed.[36]

Why is it that this struggle between an injurer's and an injured's law of torts has, up to the present time, been fought within a law of fault liability? The fact that civil liability was long part of the criminal law, which from early times has relied upon a theory of punishment for fault, does not offer a sufficient explanation because civil liability failed to discard the fault theory even after its emancipation from the criminal law;[37] nor do the influence of the Roman law or of the moral philosophy of the Church account, by themselves, for the preservation of that theory;[38] or the "natural law" doctrine whose "eternal principles" have always equally supported both a theory of fault liability and the opposite postulate "that the damage which we have in-

---

[35] See James, supra note 12, 377.

[36] Bauer, *The Degree of Moral Fault as Affecting Defendant's Liability*, 81 U. of PA. L. REV. 586 (1933). See also Bauer, *The Degree of Defendant's Fault as Affecting the Administration of the Law of Excessive Compensatory Damages*, 82 U. of PA. L. REV. 583 (1934). The separate treatment of "gross negligence" in various fields [see e.g., Eliott, *Degrees of Negligence*, 6 SO. CAL. L. REV. 91, 127 (1933)] can be traced back to the civil law doctrine. See Coggs v. Bernard, 2 Ld. Raym. 909, 92 Eng. Rep. 107 (1703). See also F. Green, *High Care and Gross Negligence*, 23 ILL. L. REV. 4 (1928). For the Continental law see Takayanagi, supra note 12, 16 ILL. L. REV. 166; EHRENZWEIG, op. cit. supra note 21, at 203 et seq. The vitality of Continental tort law in present-day Louisiana is stressed by F. F. Stone, *Tort Doctrine in Louisiana: The Materials for the Decision of a Case*, 17 TULANE L. REV. 159 (1942). See in general Green, *Illinois Negligence Law*, 39 ILL. L. REV. 36, 116, 197; 40 ILL. L. REV. 1, 47 (1944-1945).

[37] See 1 STAT. 556, 5 & 6 W. & M., c. 12 (1694), an Act to take away the process for the Capiatur fine in the several courts at Westminster. POLLOCK, TORTS (14th ed., 1939) 455 n.d.; PROSSER, TORTS 14 et seq. On the relation between criminal and civil negligence see Moreland, supra note 16, 127; Morris, *The Role of Criminal Statutes in Negligence Actions*, 49 COL. L. REV. 21 (1949).

[38] See Harris, *Liability without Fault*, 6 TULANE L. REV. 337, 349 (1932). On the history of Roman and Greek law, Radin, supra note 12, at 703.

flicted on others must be made good."[39] Rather, the fault theory has been maintained, I believe, as the governing theory of tort law because the only alternative has too often been seen in a rule of unrestricted liability for all causation. Such a rule would not only be impracticable but could be rationalized only by the paradoxical argument that the innocent injured is "still more innocent than the innocent injurer,"[40] that is by a fault theory of non-fault liability which has found a peculiar expression in Sections 403 and 404 of the Soviet Civil Code.[41] The attempt will be made in this study to show that a strict liability for all causation is not the only alternative, but that fault liability for harm foreseeably caused by reprehensible conduct can be, and as to enterprise risks has largely been, replaced by a liability for "negligence without fault" for harm typically caused by lawful conduct.

2. THE INDUSTRIAL REVOLUTION

§ 3.   a. *Harm unavoidably caused by lawful enterprise. The negligence rule rebels.* By an ironical turn of legal history the appearance and judicial recognition of mechanical enterprise as a new source of risks and losses has not only failed to produce a new principle of civil liability, but has actually played the decisive part in perfecting the fault dogma.[42] It is with the appearance and recognition of the new risks of

---

[39] LARVA LEGIS AQUILIAE DETRACTA ACTIONI DE DAMNO DATO RECEPTAE IN FORIS GERMANORUM by GAIUS MATHIAS AREND "preside Thomasio" (1743) 4. See also THOMASIUS, FUNDAMENTA JURIS NATURAE ET GENTIUM (1728) 17 § 46. In general see Isaacs, *Fault and Liability, Two Views of Legal Development*, 31 HARV. L. REV. 954 (1918).

[40] For a history and criticism of this "paradoxon" see UNGER, HANDELN AUF EIGENE GEFAHR (Acting at One's Peril) (1904).

[41] These sections impose liability for causation while permitting proof of unavoidability. See 1 GSOVSKI, SOVIET CIVIL LAW 489 (1948); *Assurance Oblige*, supra note 1, at 448.

[42] See WINFIELD, LAW OF TORT (3d ed., 1946) 391; Winfield, *The History of Negligence in the Law of Torts*, 42 L. Q. REV. 184, 195 (1926)

mechanical enterprise, that "No liability without fault" came to claim general validity. Whatever protection the injured has since achieved has been developed within legal rules couched in terms of censure for the "negligent" injurer. While this result may, if clearly realized, represent a desirable compromise, the fact that it has been concealed behind a nondiscriminating terminology has, I believe, created many of the problems and conflicts of our modern tort law.

Transportation by railroads was among the first risks of mechanical enterprise which demanded and produced a liability stricter than that for reprehensible conduct. Railroad liability to shippers for the safety of their goods fell easily into the pattern of the age-old strict liability of common carriers.[43] But the liability of railroads to their passengers has always been governed by the negligence rule previously applied to the carriage of passengers by coach.[44] This failure of the courts to extend strict liability to passengers may have been due to the fact that the rationale of the common carriers' liability[45] seemed inapplicable; that

("Perhaps one of the chief agencies in the growth of the idea is industrial machinery.") See also Green, *The Duty Problem in Negligence Cases*, 29 COL. L. REV. 255, 260 (1929); Seavey, supra note 24, 439; Marceau, *Reflections on the Theory of Negligence*, 5 LA. L. REV. 495, 496 (1944). PROSSER, TORTS 26, n.31, reports that out of 279 Minnesota cases on proximate cause, only 33 had not concerned defendants "who by means of rates, prices, taxes or insurance are best able to distribute to the public at large the risks and losses which are inevitable in a complex civilization."

[43] See 2 KENT, COMMENTARIES 602 (2d ed., 1832).

[44] See Aston v. Heaven, 2 Esp. 533, 170 Eng. Rep. 445 (1797). JONES, ESSAY ON THE LAW OF BAILMENTS (first published in 1796) mentions passenger claims for the first time in the 1836 edition. See also Crofts v. Waterhouse, 3 Bing 319, 130 Eng. Rep. 536 (1825); Ingalls v. Bills, 9 Metc. 1 (Mass. 1845). For a discussion of this "amazing" result see RAY, NEGLIGENCE OF IMPOSED DUTIES, COMMON CARRIERS 22 (1893). See also Bohlen, *Fifty Years of Torts*, 50 HARV. L. REV. 725, 727 (1937); Ballantine, *A Compensation Plan for Railway Accident Claims*, 29 HARV. L. REV. 705, 706 (1916).

[45] That liability was thought to be founded upon a custom designed to prevent carriers' frauds, and upon the consideration that "they can

at that time all strict liabilities were considered as the remnants of a barbarous age;[46] and that limitation of liability was favored by the Roman law[47] and the economic doctrine of laissez faire,[48] as well as by the desire to encourage industrial enterprise.[49] Similar reasons have probably determined the adoption of the fault theory for other enterprise liabilities.

A development towards a stricter liability cannot be observed until the second half of the nineteenth century. That development was apparently due to a certain sentiment of hostility against innovations caused by the increase of industrial risks and financial failures; to the humanitarian demand for broader protection in a more social minded era; and finally to the fact that the growing industrial wealth and stability, coupled with a spreading system of liability insurance,[50] made it easier to dispense with the injurer's

---

protect themselves" (Aston v. Heaven, supra note 44, at 535, 170 Eng. Rep. at 446), while inanimate property could not [Camden & Amboy R.R. v. Burke, 13 Wend. 611, 618 (N. Y. 1835)]. See also Christie v. Griggs, 2 Campb. 79, 170 Eng. Rep. 1088 (1809).

[46] See Camden & Amboy R.R. v. Burke, supra note 45 at 623; J. Smith, *Tort and Absolute Liability—Suggested Changes in Classification*, 30 HARV. L. REV. 241, 319, 409 (1917).

[47] The Roman law (as taught by Pothier in his *Pandects*) had greatly influenced Jones, Story, and Kent, the principal authorities referred to in the early liability cases. See Camden & Amboy R.R. v. Burke, supra note 45, at 625; KENT, op. cit. supra note 43, at 598.

[48] "Let the loss rest where it falls" seems to have been the creed of the era, also expressed in the caveat emptor of contract law [see Hamilton, *The Ancient Maxim Caveat Emptor*, 40 YALE L. J. 1133 (1931); Llewellyn, *On Warranty of Quality and Society*, 36 COL. L. REV. 699 (1936) and 37 COL. L. REV. 341 (1937)], and in the fellow-servant rule in the law of torts [see Farwell v. Boston & Worcester R. R., 4 Metc. 49, 38 Am. Dec. 339 (Mass. 1842)].

[49] This spirit was still alive in Bohlen's criticism of the *Rylands v. Fletcher* rule [Bohlen, *The Rule in Rylands v. Fletcher*, 59 U. of PA. L. REV. 298, 373, 423 (1911)] as well as in earlier aircraft cases [e.g., Herndon v. Gregory, 190 Ark. 702, 81 S. W. (2d) 849 (1935)]. But cf. Molloy, *Fletcher v. Rylands, a Reëxamination of Juristic Origins*, 9 U. of CHI. L. REV. 266 (1942); Prosser, *Nuisance Without Fault*, 20 TEX. L. REV. 399 (1942); infra § 20.

[50] See infra § 11.

protection afforded by a liability law primarily based on fault. It became more and more apparent that it was "socially expedient to spread and distribute throughout the community the inevitable losses."[51]

Here and there, this tendency has led to the enactment of strict liability statutes[52] and to stillborn theories such as that of the new liability for "ultrahazardous activities."[53] But in general the new trend has developed within the law of negligence liability, where it could not fail to transform substantially the concepts of negligence as reprehensible conduct and of negligent causation as causation of foreseeable and avoidable harm.[54] For neither the entrepreneur's lawful activity itself nor the individual causative act satisfies both requirements. A hazardous activity cannot be penalized as "reprehensible" if lawful; and the harm caused in the course of that lawful activity is not "avoidable" if calculated as unavoidable at the start of that activity.[55]

---

[51] Y. B. Smith, supra note 24, 457 (with reference to employee claims). See also, e.g., Feezer, *Social Justice in the Field of Torts*, 11 MINN. L. REV. 313 (1927); Feezer, *Capacity to Bear Loss as a Factor in the Decision of Certain Types of Tort Cases*, 78 U. of PA. L. REV. 805 (1930); *Assurance Oblige*, supra note 1, at 446.

[52] See e.g., the Uniform Aeronautics Act, 11 U.L.A. 159 (1938) adopted in at least 20 states. See in general Takayanagi, supra note 12, 270 et seq. On the Continent of Europe legal writers have long demanded the recognition of a general principle of liability for hazardous activities [see, e.g., RANDA, DIE SCHADENERSATZPFLICHT (2d ed. 1908)]; and statutes have adopted this liability for specific "dangerous enterprises" such as railroads, automobiles, aircraft, and suppliers of electricity. In a significant decision (Sept. 10, 1947, 1 Ob 500/47) the Supreme Court of Austria has used such statutes to establish a doctrine of respondeat superior (otherwise foreign to Continental law) for hazardous activities. See Fenzl, *Erfolgshaftung der "Gefaehrlichen Betriebe,"* 3 OESTERREICHISCHE JURISTENZEITUNG 362 (1948).

[53] See Rest. Torts, § 519; Comment, *Absolute Liability for Ultrahazardous Activities: An Appraisal of the Restatement Doctrine*, 37 CALIF. L. REV. 269 (1949) with further references.

[54] See infra § 9.

[55] Similar problems have arisen for similar reasons under laws which, though excusing trespass in emergency, impose damages on the trespasser. See the writer's IRRTUM UND RECHTSWIDRIGKEIT (Mistake and Unlawfulness) 21 (Vienna: 1931); infra Part II note 38.

Continental laws have sought to overcome similar difficulties by presumptions of fault.[56] "Where one would not or could not change the substantive law, the procedural law was used and the victim was assisted by . . . a presumption of fault."[57] American law, whose pioneer spirit was probably opposed to thus stigmatizing growing enterprise, has reached similar results by adopting two rules which have hidden the subservience to the needs of our era behind foreign words simulating ancient origin.

§ 4.   b. *Respondeat superior and res ipsa loquitur. The rule is conquered.* A man was killed in a house by gas escaping from a leak in a gas main more than 400 feet away. Judge, jury, and plaintiff will be reluctant to hold for this accident, which was of a type calculable and calculated as an unavoidable incident of the employer's enterprise, the laborer who had "negligently" encased the leaking main almost one year earlier. But, says the law, let the master answer for the servant: Respondeat superior.[58] And if we have difficulty in

---

[56] See Harris, supra note 38, 337 et seq.; *Loss-Shifting* 735; MAIORCA, PROBLEMI DELLA RESPONSABILITA' CIVILE (1936); RHEINSTEIN, THE LAW OF TORTS, CASES AND MATERIALS FROM COMMON LAW AND CIVIL LAW COUNTRIES (1940); and the writer's A NEW LAW OF TORTS (ZUR ERNEUERUNG DES SCHADENERSATZRECHTES) (1937).

[57] Société des Nations, *Institut International de Rome pour l'Unification du Droit Privé, Responsabilité Civile des Automobilistes, Étude Préliminaire* 14 (1935) (transl.).

[58] For a discussion of the function of this doctrine in the development of enterprise liability see Holmes, *Agency*, 4 HARV. L. REV. 345 (1891); Y. B. Smith, supra note 24, 460; Note, *Vicarious Liability: Statutes as a Guide to its Basis*, 45 HARV. L. REV. 171 (1931); Steffen, *Independent Contractor and the Good Life*, 2 U. of CHI. L. REV. 501, 507 (1935); PROSSER, TORTS 472. Neuner, *Respondeat Superior in the Light of Comparative Law*, 4 LA. L. REV. 1 (1941) describes the parallel development of the German law which, though clearly requiring fault (in selection or control) for vicarious liability, comes very close to the strict liability of Anglo-American and French law. See also supra note 52; Radin, supra note 12, 707. The law of Louisiana stands between the two legal systems. See Miller, *The Master-Servant Concept and Judge-Made Law*, 1 LOYOLA L. REV. 25 (1941). The law of parental liability [see Spence, *Parental Liability*, [1948] INS. L. J. 787 (1948)] and the "family car doctrine"

finding fault with the servant, let the thing speak for itself: Res ipsa loquitur.[59] Let the thing help the victim in proving that something has occurred in the master's hazardous activities that can justly be imputed to the master. If we may trust hesitant beginnings, the thing may yet come to stand by itself for such proof.[60]

By two bold strokes, negligence liability has thus been enabled to distribute the losses caused by modern enterprise. But the resulting strict liability, having preserved the language and limitations of the law of negligence, lacks a rationale. *This* negligence liability is not liability for avoidable causation by reprehensible conduct of foreseeable harm. True, respondeat superior, too, though rendering liable a nonnegligent employer, purports to be based on negligent causation requiring foreseeability of harm. But could the laborer who encased the leaking gas main, or any reasonable man in his place, in that split second of inattentiveness in which he committed his technical error, in any real sense foresee harm such as the stranger's death one year later? If foreseeability is understood as a psychological reality rather than a legal fiction, a negative answer seems obvious; and yet the highest court of New York held the laborer's employer for negligence.[61] True, respondeat superior too, though creating a liability for harm arising from lawful activities, purports to be based on reprehensible conduct. But was the children's drowning in the frozen pond reprehensibly caused by that (unidentified and perhaps unidentifiable) foreman for whose action we want to hold the railroad? A negative answer seems obvious, and yet a jury found negligence, a trial court assessed damages and two appellate

[James, supra note 9, 564] offer interesting analogies. See infra § 20. See also Ferson, *Bases for Master's Liability and for Principal's Liability to Third Persons*, 4 VAND. L. REV. 260, 263 (1951).

[59] For history, rationale, and principal applications of this doctrine, as well as for further references see PROSSER, TORTS 293, and Prosser, *Res Ipsa Loquitur in California*, 37 CALIF. L. REV. 183 (1949). See also Note, 47 COL. L. REV. 850 (1947).

[60] See infra § 8 at note 128.

[61] See Ehret v. Village of Scarsdale, 269 N. Y. 198, 199 N. E. 56 (1935).

judges agreed.[62] Perhaps it is signficant for the imperceptible shift of the negligence concept from reprehensible causative conduct to lawful enterprise activity that in both cases the court, unwillingly perhaps, spoke of the "defendant's" foresight rather than that of its employee.

The Supreme Court of the United States, in a long line of cases under the Federal Employers Liability Act[63] has permitted jury verdicts against railroads for common law negligence to stand in the absence of such reprehensible conduct or foreseeable harm as would probably have been required against non-enterprise defendants—as in the case of the switchman who fell into defendant's pit, though posts and chains had been erected to prevent employees from entering the area.[64] Mr. Justice Frankfurter states that the difficulties in these cases derive "largely from the outmoded concept of 'negligence' as a working principle for the adjustments of injuries inevitable under the technological circumstances of modern industry."[65] Perhaps we are adhering here to a "cruel and wasteful mode of dealing with industrial injuries,"[66] which should and will ultimately be replaced by statute. But much of the present confusion can probably be removed by realizing that the law of negligence as applied in this field has undergone a fundamental change in its constituent concepts of the "reasonable man" and his "foresight." Before a general analysis of this problem can

---

[62] Irwin Savings & Trust Co. v. Pa. R. R., supra note 2.

[63] See the summary of these cases in Justice Douglas' concurring opinion in Wilkerson v. McCarthy, 336 U. S. 53, 68, 69 Sup. Ct. 413, 420 (1949).

[64] Wilkerson v. McCarthy, supra note 63. See also, e.g., Anderson v. Atchison, T. & S. F. R. R., 333 U.S. 821, 68 Sup. Ct. 854 (1948) (conductor dying from injuries after having fallen off the train,—no allegation that crew knew of fall or injuries or that fall caused by defendant's negligence); Urie v. Thompson, 337 U. S. 163, 69 Sup. Ct. 1018 (1949) (occupational disease); supra note 4.

[65] Wilkerson v. McCarthy, supra note 63, at 65, 69 Sup. Ct. at 419. See also Mr. Justice Frankfurter's concurring opinion in Urie v. Thompson, supra note 64 at 196, 69 Sup. Ct. at 1038.

[66] Wilkerson v. McCarthy, supra note 63 at 65, 69 Sup. Ct. at 419.

be made, a brief survey of the fields of its appearance seems in order.

3. SOME "NEGLIGENT" ENTREPRENEURS

§ 5.   a. *Transportation, utilities, and entertainment.* In the law of *railroad* liability to passengers various devices have been used from the beginning to promote a stricter liability. Early courts, in order to be able to hold a railroad for injuries caused by a defective axle, treated the manufacturer as the railroad's "agent" and borrowed a theory of "warranty of roadworthiness" from the law of the sea.[67] The later development, however, was entirely based on a theory of respondeat superior for negligence. Indeed, "the law of negligence of the late nineteenth century was to a considerable extent the law of railway accidents."[68] The growth of railroad liability under this doctrine can be followed through the several editions of Story's famous textbook on bailments. The first edition (1832) declares it as "certain" that carriers with regard to their passengers "are bound only to due care and diligence in the performance of their duty."[69] The third edition (1843), citing the first railroad cases, adds that "of course" carriers are responsible "for any, even the slightest neglect," and introduces a presumption of fault.[70] The sixth

---

[67] Hegeman v. Western R. R., 3 Kernan (13 N.Y.) 9, 22 (1855). Accord: Alden v. N. Y. C. R. R., 26 N. Y. 102, 104 (1862), stressing the advantage of the certainty of this "hard rule" over the "trouble and expense of a strongly litigated contest before juries." But cf. McPadden v. N. Y. C. R. R., 44 N. Y. 478 (1871). On the doctrine of seaworthiness see the excellent Note, 34 CORN. L. Q. 92 (1948).

[68] Prosser, *Res Ipsa Loquitur in California,* 37 CALIF. L. REV. 183, 186 (1949).

[69] STORY, COMMENTARIES ON THE LAW OF BAILMENTS 378 (1832).

[70] Id. (3d ed., 1843) at 592: "For the law will . . . in tenderness to human life and human limbs, hold the proprietors liable for the slightest negligence, and will compel them to repel, by satisfactory proofs, every imputation thereof" (at 593). A significant phase of the development of railroad liability in Illinois is described by Green, supra note 36, 39 ILL. L. REV. 36, 42 et seq.

edition (1856) is the first one expressly to discuss railroad liability and, significantly enough, the first one to talk in terms of risk and public policy: "When carriers undertake to convey persons by the powerful but dangerous agency of steam, public policy and safety require that they be held to the greatest possible care and diligence."[71] In conjunction with this rule, the railroad's burden of proof has carried the railroad's stricter liability into many other fields of the law of torts,[72] by "cross-breeding" with the rule of res ipsa loquitur in its original meaning as a rule of evidence.[73]

In the law of *automobile* liability, as in the law of railroad liability, an inherently dangerous activity was made lawful because of a prevailing social interest.[74] Early attempts to subject the "devil wagon" to the rule applying to "ferocious animals"[75] failed, apparently because such strict liability had never been established for railroads. But here, as in the law of railroads, the application of negligence liability to the inevitable results of a lawful activity has deprived the negligence test of its original meaning; the foresight of the

---

[71] STORY, op. cit, supra note 69, at 607, quoting from Pha. and Reading R. R. v. Derby, 14 How. (55 U.S.) 468, 486 (1852). Significant summaries of railroad cases are now currently published in the NACCA LAW JOURNAL. See, e.g., vol. 1, at 153 and vol. 2, at 245.

[72] See Scott v. London & St. Katherine Docks Co., 3 H. & C. 596, 601, 159 Eng. Rep. 665, 667 (1865); Prosser, supra note 68 at 184.

[73] See Prosser, supra note 68 at 186, 187.

[74] To use Terry's terminology, a "negligent conduct" ceased to be a "negligent wrong" because of the "necessity of the risk." See infra § 20.

[75] Lewis v. Amorous, 3 Ga. App. 50, 55, 59 S. E. 338, 340 (1907). In 1904 we read complaints about "wealthy hoodlums" with their "devil wagons." Note, 59 CENT. L. J. 432 (1904). In 1909 an automobile was declared to be "nearly as deadly as, and much more dangerous than, a street car or even a railroad car" [Weil v. Kreutzer, 134 Ky. 563, 567, 121 S. W. 471, 472 (1909)]; and as late as 1920, the Florida court treated the automobile as a dangerous instrumentality rendering the owner liable whenever negligently used [Southern Cotton Oil Co. v. Anderson, 80 Fla. 441, 86 So. 629 (1920)]. See also PROSSER, TORTS 500; James, supra note 9, 564; Blakemore, *Is the Law Fair to the Motor Vehicle?* 65 U.S.L. REV. 20 (1931); Nixon, *Changing Rules of Liability in Automobile Accident Litigation,* 3 LAW & CONTEMP. PROB. 476 (1936).

reasonable man, with or without the help of res ipsa, has come to be applied to innocent, and even to involuntary, acts.[76] And the "family car" doctrine or owners' liability statutes[77] have effected shifts similar to those effected by the doctrine of respondeat superior in other fields of enterprise liability.

The liability of *air carriers*, after a start in the direction of an absolute liability similar to that for ferocious animals and explosives,[78] has apparently returned to the general negligence rule and its problems.[79] Here, too, the doctrine of res ipsa loquitur may yet become the vehicle of a stricter liability,[80] unless occasional deviations from negligence language foreshadow the beginnings of a more articulate theory of

---

[76] See Loss-Shifting, supra note 1, 739; BOWERS, SELECTED ARTICLES ON COMPULSORY INSURANCE 36 (1929); FRENCH, THE AUTOMOBILE COMPENSATION PLAN 46 (1933); SPILREIN, LE CONTRAT D'ASSURANCE DE RESPONSABILITÉ CIVILE (1934) 11, 18; Nixon, supra note 75, 477 ("fractional mistake in management"); Barret, *Mechanics of Control and Lookout in Automobile Law*, 14 TULANE L. REV. 493 (1940). The INSURANCE LAW JOURNAL publishes currently significant automobile cases.

[77] See James, supra note 9, 564; infra § 20.

[78] Guille v. Swan, 19 Johns. 381, 10 Am. Dec. 234 (N.Y. 1822) (forced landing in private garden); Canney v. Rochester Agricultural and Mechanical Ass'n, 76 N. H. 60, 79 Atl. 517 (1911) (falling balloon). Cf. McNAIR, THE LAW OF THE AIR (1932); Kingsley and Bates, *Liability to Persons and Property on the Ground*, 4 J. of AIR L. 515 (1933).

[79] Richmond & M. Ry. Co. v. Moore, 94 Va. 493, 27 S. E. 70 (1897); Peckett v. Bergen Beach Co., 44 App. Div. 559, 60 N. Y. Supp. 966 (1899); Roper v. Ulster Co. Agric. Soc., 136 App. Div. 97, 120 N. Y. Supp. 644 (1909); Platt v. Erie Co. Agric. Soc., 164 App. Div. 99, 149 N. Y. Supp. 520 (1914). For further references see Bohlen, *Aviation Under the Common Law*, 48 HARV. L. REV. 216 (1934); RHYNE, AVIATION ACCIDENT LAW (1943).

[80] See Smith v. Pennsylvania Central Airlines Corp., 76 F. Supp. 940 (D. C., 1948). For other authorities for and against the application of the doctrine see Note, 16 U. of CHI. L. REV. 365, 367 (1949); Goldin, *The Doctrine of Res Ipsa Loquitur in Aviation Law*, 18 SO. CAL. L. REV. 15, 124 (1944); O'Connor, *Res Ipsa in the Air*, 22 IND. L. J. 221 (1947); McLarty, *Res Ipsa Loquitur Doctrine in Airline Passenger Litigation*, 37 VA. L. REV. 55 (1951); Note, 28 N. C. L. REV. 432 (1950).

risk distribution.[81] The Warsaw Convention[82] and suggestions for similar federal and uniform state legislation[83] seem to point towards the adoption of non-fault compensation schemes. Corresponding developments can be observed in the liability of suppliers of telephone and telegraph service, of *electricity*[84] and of oil and *gas*.[85] And there seems to be a definite trend toward an increased "fault" liability of public entertainers[86] and innkeepers.[87]

§ 6.   b. *Immune entrepreneurs* (governmental subdivisions, charities, and trusts). The ancient maxim that "the King can do no wrong" has long proved inappropriate where the "King" has come to compete with private enterprise and where enterprise liability is not related to a "wrong" done. But, after initial attempts at abolishing the immunity rule,[88]

---

[81] See, e.g., Rochester Gas & Elec. Corp. v. Dunlop, 148 Misc. 849, 852, 266 N. Y. Supp. 469, 473 (1933): "Such chance as there may be that a properly equipped and well handled aeroplane may still crash . . . shall be borne by him who takes the machine aloft."

[82] C. III, Art. 22, 49 STAT. 3019 (1935). Cf. Rhyne, *International Law and Air Transportation*, 47 MICH. L. REV. 41 (1948).

[83] See Uniform Aeronautics Act, 11 U. L. A. 173 (1938); Note, 16 U. of CHI. L. REV. 365, 371 (1949); Coblentz, *Limitation of Liability for Aircraft*, 23 SO. CAL. L. REV. 473 (1950).

[84] See Harvin, *Liability of Electric Company for Personal Injuries*, [1947] INS. L. J. 794 (1947); Challener, *Injuries Incident to the Production and Use of Electricity in Pennsylvania*, 24 TEMPLE L. Q. 42 (1950).

[85] See Tipton, *Liability of a Gas Company for Personal Injuries*, [1948] INS. L. J. 275 (1948).

[86] See, e.g., Wells v. Palm Beach Kennel Club, 35 So. (2d) 720 (Fla. 1948) (patron at dog race track slipping on grandstand); Rafter v. Dubrock's Riding Academy, 75 C. A. (2d) 621, 171 P. (2d) 459 (1946); Salevan v. Wilmington Park, 72 A. (2d) 239 (Del. Super. 1950) (pedestrian hit by baseball from adjoining ball park); PROSSER, TORTS § 79; Note, 47 MICH. L. REV. 588 (1949).

[87] See Steinfeld, *The Hotel—Always the Insurer*, [1947] INS. L. J. 316 (1947). See also Maryland v. Manor Real Estate & Trust Co. et al., 176 F. (2d) 414 (4th Cir. 1949) ("Negligence" liability of U.S. Government as lessor of apartment house); and for a warehouse liability case George v. Bekins Van & Storage Co., 33 Cal. (2d) 834, 205 P. (2d) 1037 (1949).

[88] See, e.g., Hooe v. Alexandria, 1 Cr. C. C. 98, 12 Fed. Cas. No. 6667 (U.S.C.C.) (1802).

fear of exposing *governmental enterprise* to intolerable burdens at the taxpayer's expense has enabled that rule to withstand the general advance of corporate liability. Thus, for a long time, governmental liability was limited to "proprietary" activities and to what purported to be a strict liability for nuisance.[89] More recently, however, dissatisfaction with artificial distinctions and the enormous growth of governmental activities has caused the extension of governmental liability by such statutory enactments as the Federal Tort Claims Act,[90] by voluntary recognition of a "moral obligation"[91] and by the spread and recognition of "liability" insurance for immune activities.[92] But neither the old immunity rule nor its abolition can take account of the fact that losses caused by governmental enterprise may require distribution either among its beneficiaries or among taxpayers, or of the fact that the doctrine of respondeat superior as the enterprise liability vehicle of the law of negligence, is

---

[89] See, e.g., Bingham v. Board of Education of Ogden City,—Utah—, 223 P. (2d) 432, 438 (1950); cases collected in 156 A.L.R. 692, 714 (1945); Barnett, *The Foundation of the Distinction between Public and Private Functions in Respect to the Common-Law Tort Liability of Municipal Corporations*, 16 ORE. L. REV. 250 (1937). The theory of nuisance carried municipal tort liability for a considerable period. See Warp, *The Law and Administration of Municipal Tort Liability*, 28 VA. L. REV. 360, 367 (1942); Peterson, *Governmental Responsibility for Torts in Minnesota*, 26 MINN. L. REV. 293, 480, 613, 700, 854 (1942); Fuller-Casner, *Municipal Tort Liability in Operation*, 54 HARV. L. REV. 437 (1941). More recently the law of nuisance seems to have lost its independent significance. See PROSSER, TORTS 553; Winfield, Nuisance as a Tort, 4 CAMB. L. J. 189 (1930); POTTER, PRINCIPLES OF LIABILITY IN TORT 37 (1948).

[90] 60 Stat. 842, 28 U.S.C.A. § 921. See Comment, *The Courts and the Federal Tort Claims Act*, 98 PA. L. REV. 884 (1950). For a typical state statute see the New York Court of Claims Act, Laws 1939, p. 2178, 2181 c. 860, § 8.

[91] See Note, 33 MINN. L. REV. 634, 637 n.13 (1949).

[92] See, e.g., 1 Minn. Stat. § 125.0656 (1945) (authorization of school districts to insure); Rogers v. Butler, 170 Tenn. 125, 92 S.W. (2nd) 414 (1936) (waiver of immunity by insurance); La Mourea v. Rhude, 209 Minn. 53, 295 N.W. 304 (1940) (recovery against insurer of immune tortfeasor under third party beneficiary contract theory); infra note 98. Cf. James and Thornton, supra note 9, at 438.

wholly inadequate if applied to public employee "wrong-doers" in what should be a domain of public law.[93] These and other considerations have prompted the demand for a statutory compensation scheme.[94] Here too, however, I believe, that a new analysis of the law of enterprise "negligence" could bring relief without legislative interference.

Tort liability of *charities* is, in the words of Mr. Justice Rutledge, characterized by "paradoxes of principle, fictional assumptions of fact and consequence, and confused results."[95] The common law rule of immunity can no longer be supported by a traditional rationale[96] and has "become merely a relic in the multitude of departures."[97] Though most jurisdictions nevertheless adhere to that rule, the availability of liability insurance, having virtually removed the need for the protection of the "trust fund" against tort claims,[98]

[93] See the writer's *Soldiers' Liability for Wrongs Committed on Duty*, 30 CORN. L. Q. 179 (1944); FAIRMAN, THE LAW OF MARTIAL RULE 313 (1943); and in general DAVID, THE TORT LIABILITY OF PUBLIC OFFICERS (1940). On a possible criminal liability of the Crown, see Friedmann, *Public Welfare Offences, Statutory Duties, and the Legal Status of the Crown*, 13 MOD. L. REV. 24 (1950).

[94] See Lloyd, *Municipal Tort Liability in New York—A Legislative Challenge*, 23 N. Y. U. L. Q. REV. 278 (1948); Lloyd, *Le Roi est Mort; Vive le Roi*, 24 N. Y. U. L. Q. REV. 38 (1949); and in general SYMPOSIUM, GOVERNMENTAL TORT LIABILITY, 9 LAW & CONTEMP. PROB. 179 (1942); Green, *Municipal Liability for Torts*, 38 ILL. L. REV. 355 (1944); Borchard, *Tort Claims against Government: Municipal, State and Federal Liability*, 33 A. B. A. J. 221 (1947). An important new phase of the problem is discussed in Knauth, *Government Liability for Aircraft Damage*, 37 ILL. L. REV. 355 (1944); Borchard, *Tort Claims against Government: Municipal, State and Federal Liability*, 33 A. B. A. J. 221 (1947).

[95] President and Directors of Georgetown College v. Hughes, 130 F. (2d) 810, 812 (D. C. 1942).

[96] See, e.g., Powers v. Mass. Homeopathic Hosp., 109 Fed. 294 (C.C.A. 1st, 1901) (waiver by beneficiary); Southern Methodist Hosp. & San. v. Wilson, 45 Ariz. 507, 46 P. (2d) 118 (1935) (inapplicability of respondeat superior); Lindler v. Columbia Hosp., 98 S. C. 25, 81 S. E. 512 (1914) (public policy); infra note 98 ("trust fund" doctrine). For a good compilation see Comment, 2 VAND. L. REV. 660 (1949).

[97] President and Directors of Georgetown College v. Hughes, supra note 95, at 817.

[98] See Wendt v. Servite Fathers, 332 Ill. App. 618, 76 N. E. (2d) 342 (1947); Note, 43 ILL. L. REV. 248 (1947); [1948] INS. L. J. 120 (1948).

may ultimately result in the abandonment of the immunity of charitable enterprise, if and when the resulting liability for enterprise negligence has found a new rationale. The same expectation may be justified regarding the intra-family immunity which still purports to preserve the "amity of domestic relations"[99] where ultimate liability rests on the insurer rather than on the father or spouse.[100]

Trusts and corporations, like charitable institutions, have often been used to protect entrepreneurs from an unlimited liability likely to impair daring and initiative. But the immunity of shareholder and estate will hardly survive the impact of liability insurance any longer than the immunity of governmental and charitable enterprise. While pertinent developments in the law of corporations probably do not yet permit conclusive discussion,[101] the immunity of entrepreneur trust estates seems decisively affected by recoveries

See also O'Connor v. Boulder Ass'n, 105 Colo. 259, 96 P. (2d) 835 (1939); Vanderbilt University v. Henderson, 23 Tenn. App. 135, 127 S.W. (2d) 284 (1938) [cited with approval Baptist Memorial Hosp. v. Couillens, 176 Tenn. 300, 140 S.W. (2d) 1088 (1940), and Anderson v. Armstrong, 180 Tenn. 56, 171 S.W. (2d) 401 (1943); Andrews v. Y.M.C.A., 228 Iowa 374, 410, 284 N.W. 187, 205 (1939), quoted with approval Foster v. Roman Catholic Diocese of Vermont, 116 Vt. 76, 70 A. (2d) 230 (1950); Moore v. Moyle, 405 Ill. 555, 92 N.E. (2d) 81 (1950). A similar problem has arisen with regard to governmental liabilities. See Pohland v. Sheboygan, 251 Wis. 20, 27 N.W. (2d) 736 (1947). The "trust fund" doctrine seems to have originated in a dictum of Lord Cottenham in Feoffees of Heriot's Hosp. v. Ross, 12 C. & F. 507, 513, 8 Eng. Rep. 1508, 1510 (1846).

[99] Shumaker, *Action for Tort between Husband and Wife,* 30 LAW NOTES 165 (1926). See also Haglund, *Tort Actions between Husband and Wife,* 27 GEO. L. J. 697, 893 (1939); James and Thornton, supra note 9, at 434; and infra note 154.

[100] See, e.g., Dunlap v. Dunlap, 84 N. H. 352, 150 Atl. 905 (1930). See also dissents in McKinney v. McKinney, 59 Wyo. 204, 247, 135 P. (2d) 940, 956 (1943) and Cowgill v. Boock,—Ore.—, 218 P. (2d) 445, 458 (1950). The statutory abolition of "no action" clauses in insurance contracts (excluding the insurer's liability for noncollectible claims against an insolvent insured) is another expression of this trend. See James and Thornton, supra note 9, at 436.

[101] Inroads in that immunity are theories such as those of ultra vires, abuse of voting power or dangerous corporate activity.

against them of trustees and even of third parties, under tests which, I believe, support the classification of negligence liabilities here suggested.[102]

§ 7.   c. *Products liability.* The development of tort law from rudimentary strict liabilities and a general liability for negligence towards compensation and loss distribution can perhaps be best observed in the changing pattern of the products liability of manufacturers and other sellers.[103] As to food sales, considerations of public health led to the early adoption of strict liabilities based on penal statutes or implied warranties of wholesomeness.[104] But as to other sales there prevailed until the nineteenth century "the legal presumption of the buyer's ability to look out for himself," generally formulated in the maxim of caveat emptor.[105] Limitation of the buyer's relief to the breach of express warranties was deemed "best calculated to excite the caution and attention which all prudent men ought to observe in making

---

[102] See Uniform Trusts Act, Sec. 14, 9 U. L. A. 719, adopted in five states; and in general, Fulda and Pond, *Tort Liability of Trust Estates,* 41 COL. L. REV. 1332 (1941); infra § 21.

[103] See PROSSER, TORTS 666 et seq.; *Products Liability,* supra note 1, and the writer's Note, 8 U. of CHI. L. REV. 162 (1940). The term "products liability," though generally used in the literature of insurance business [see WIGGERS, PRODUCTS LIABILITY INSURANCE (1931); KRAJIRIK, COURT DECISIONS ON PRODUCTS LIABILITY (1941)], has been used only hesitatingly in legal literature. But see, e.g., Lewis, *Theories of Action in Products Liability Litigation,* [1947] INS. L. J. 30 (1947); Robb, *A Storekeeper's Liability,* [1948] INS. L. J. 489, 491 (1948).

[104] See Morris, *The Relation of Criminal Statutes to Tort Liability,* 46 HARV. L. REV. 453 (1933); Thaler, *Liability for Sale of Impure Foods,* 11 BROOKLYN L. REV. 209 (1942); *Products Liability,* supra note 1, §§ 3 ff. The theory of implied warranty, based upon a passage in Blackstone [3 COMMENTARIES 165 (ed. Lewis, 1900)] and appearing in New York as early as 1815 [Van Bracklin v. Fonda, 12 Johns. 468] and 1837 [dissent in Wright v. Hart, 18 Wend. 449, 455] has become the law in most jurisdictions. See Prosser, *The Implied Warranty of Merchantable Quality,* 27 MINN. L. REV. 117, 118, 132 (1943).

[105] Hamilton, *The Ancient Maxim Caveat Emptor,* 40 YALE L. J. 1133, 1135 (1931). See also MELICK, THE SALE OF FOOD AND DRINK (1936).

their contracts."[106] Even the Uniform Sales Act, adopted in most jurisdictions, while extensively relying on implied warranties,[107] limited protection by various requirements such as declaration of purpose, reliance, and privity. Judicial attempts at escaping these limitations by presumptions and statutory construction[108] have been only partly successful and have rarely been supported by legislation.[109] Though the need has been for compensation of the victim of the inevitable incidents of modern enterprise, the victim's protection has—here as elsewhere—largely developed within a rule of liability for fault.[110]

From *Winterbottom v. Wright*[111] with its argument in ter-

---

[106] Seixas v. Woods, 2 Caines 48, 54 (N. Y. 1804). See also 2 KENT, COMMENTARIES ON AMERICAN LAW 478, 490, 491 (4th ed., 1840).

[107] 1 U. L. A. 103, § 15. See Comment, *Should the Doctrine of Implied Warranties be Limited to Sales Transactions?*, 2 VAND. L. REV. 675 (1949).

[108] See Rinaldi v. The Mohican Co., 225 N. Y. 70, 121 N. E. 471 (1918) (presumption of declaration of purpose and reliance); Leidy, *Another New Tort?*, 38 MICH. L. REV. 964, 983 (1940); *Products Liability*, supra note 1, § 7; Klein v. Duchess Sandwich Co., 14 Cal. (2d) 272, 283, 93 P. (2d) 799, 804 (1939) ("clear intent of the legislature"). See also the excellent discussion of these and other "fictions" by Justice Traynor in Escola v. Coca-Cola Bottling Co., 24 Cal. (2d) 453, 465, 150 P. (2d) 436, 442 (1944).

[109] See Conn. (1939) Supplement to Gen. Stat. c. 232 (Pub. Acts § 186) § 1276. (e), overruling Borucki v. MacKenzie Bros. Co., 125 Conn. 92, 3 A. (2d) 224 (1938) and extending the consumer's protection to "all members of the buyer's household." Similar proposals in New York [e.g., (1943) Sen. Int. No. 224, Pr. No. 226, Assembly Int. No. 216, Pr. No. 218] have apparently little chance of overcoming the ill-considered resistance of insurers. Section 2-318 of the Uniform Commercial Code (Spring, 1950, Draft) would extend all express and implied warranties "to any natural person who is in the family or household of the buyer or who is his guest or one whose relationship to him is such as to make it reasonable to expect that such person may use, consume or be affected by the goods."

[110] See, e.g., Llewellyn, *On Warranty of Quality and Society*, 36 COL. L. REV. 699 (1936); Winfield, *The History of Negligence in the Law of Torts*, 42 L. Q. REV. 184 (1926); Seefeld, *Tort Liability of Manufacturers to Users of Their Goods*, 25 MARQ. L. REV. 173 (1941); Morrow, *Warranty of Quality: A Comparative Survey*, 14 TULANE L. REV. 327, 529 (1940).

[111] 10 M. & W. 109, 11 L. J. Ex. 415, 152 Eng. Rep. 402 (1842).

rorem against third party recovery, through *Thomas v. Winchester*[112] with its "inherent danger" formula, a wellknown chain of judicial law making has led to *MacPherson v. Buick Motor Co.*[113] with its general negligence liability for articles "dangerous if negligently made." This rule has been adopted and developed in most jurisdictions and included in Section 395 of the Restatement of Torts. However, if inducement of producers to prevent "negligence" in their enterprises has ever been a ground for this rule, it has lost its meaning at a time when, with the spread of liability insurance, the sanction of the rule has, in general, dwindled to a mere threat of increased insurance premiums.[114] Moreover, once loss distribution through the insurer is recognized as an essential function of the products liability of the MacPherson rule, that liability should no longer be withheld from large groups of articles and interests.[115]

§ 8.   d. *Other liabilities.* Ever since the House of Lords held a newspaper liable for damage innocently done to the reputation of Artemus Jones by a presumably fictitious story,[116] strict liability has been imposed for the publication in print or in writing of a defamatory statement. This rule has been much criticized as impairing freedom of speech, promoting strike suits, and unnecessarily placing words "in the same class with the use of explosives or the keeping of dangerous animals."[117] In view of similar criticism as to

[112] 6 N. Y. 397, 57 Am. Dec. 455 (1852).

[113] 217 N. Y. 382, 11 N. E. 1050 (1916). For an illuminating analysis of this development see Levi, *An Introduction to Legal Reasoning,* 15 U. of CHI. L. REV. 501, 572 (1948).

[114] See Sawyer, *Compensation Rates and Safety,* 42 BEST'S No. 2, 47 (1941); and in general the brilliant discussion of the "impact of liability insurance" on tort law by James, supra note 9, 557 et seq.

[115] For an analysis of the law of New York in this respect see the writer's *Products Liability,* supra note 1. For a recent extension of the rule see Foley v. Pittsburgh-Des Moines Co., 363 Pa. 1, 68 A. (2d) 517 (1949) (realty). Cf. La Rocca v. Farrington, 301 N. Y. 247, 93 N. E. (2d) 829 (1950).

[116] Hulton & Co. v. Jones, [1909] 2 K. B. 444, aff'd [1910] A. C. 20.

[117] PROSSER, TORTS 817. See also Donnelly, *The Law of Defama-*

radio broadcasts, return to the negligence rule, otherwise applicable only to mere "disseminators," has been advocated and occasionally adopted, at least with regard to "ad libs" as distinguished from prepared texts. Thus, in *Kelly v. Hoffman* a public official accused in a radio broadcast of malfeasance, was denied recovery against the broadcasting company which had leased its facilities to the broadcaster's employer, because the defendant "could not have prevented publication by the exercise of reasonable care."[118] Under this theory a broadcasting company would, in effect, be liable only where it has "failed to exercise reasonable care to see to it that no scandalmonger should take advantage of its facilities."[119] It is submitted that analogous application of the "negligence" tests developed for other dangerous enterprise activities may produce a more effective protection of the public, without imposing an excessive strict liability. Here, too, the availability of liability insurance should greatly influence the tort rule.[120]

That the need for a new type of enterprise liability for "negligence without fault" is not limited to the problems discussed, may be illustrated by two additional examples from diverse fields of tort law. Modern business requires ever increasing reliance on expert certifications such as those of public accountants, notaries, title abstractors, food inspectors, and various public officers. Fear of overextend-

---

tion: Proposals for Reform, 33 MINN. L. REV. 609, 613 (1949); Note, *Television and Torts,* 15 MO. L. REV. 48 (1950); Note, *Libel and Slander; Defamation by Television,* 3 OKLA. L. REV. 446 (1950).

[118] 137 N. J. L. 695, 702, 61 A. (2d) 143, 147 (1948). See also REST. TORTS, Sec. 581, comment f (1938); Summit Hotel Co. v. National Broadcasting Co., 336 Pa. 182, 8 A. (2d) 302 (1939); Josephson v. Knickerbocker Broadcasting Co., 179 Misc. 787, 38 N. Y. S. (2d) 985 (Sup. Ct. 1942).

[119] Kelly v. Hoffman, supra note 118 at 702, 61 A. (2d) at 147, quoting with approval from Bohlen, *Fifty Years of Torts,* 50 HARV. L. REV. 725, 731 (1937).

[120] Such insurance has been written since 1930 by the Employers Reinsurance Corporation of Kansas City, Missouri. See Donnelly, *Defamation by Radio: A Reconsideration,* 34 IOWA L. REV. 12, 21 n.43 (1948) with further references.

ing the certifier's liability has probably prompted the courts to adhere to the doctrine of the *Ultramares* case[121] in which negligence liability was denied as to a plaintiff whose reliance the defendant had not contemplated. Though such plaintiffs might be protected where the defendant's negligence is serious enough to amount to "deceit,"[122] there remain the many other cases in which recovery is now denied against business enterprises inviting general reliance. Perhaps a new type of negligence liability "without fault," based on insurability, could fill the gap now only partly and unsatisfactorily covered by actions in warranty and deceit.[123]

As a final illustration for the virtually unlimited scope of the problem, reference may be made to the decision in *Summers v. Tice*,[124] holding jointly liable in negligence two members of a hunting party one of whom had negligently shot the plaintiff. This decision has been criticized for relying on a shift of the burden to prove causation.[125] But perhaps this shift does not go far enough in that the plaintiff is still required to prove the defendants' negligent conduct beyond the creation by them of risks inherent in their common hazardous activity.[126] Abandonment of this requirement and recognition in such cases of an enterprise liability for harm typically and insurably caused may be fore-

---

[121] Ultramares Corporation v. Touche, 255 N. Y. 170, 174 N. E. 441 (1931). See in general Note, *Cases on Accountants' Liability in New York*, 1 INTRAMURAL L. REV. OF N. Y. U. 57 (1945); Harper and McNeely, *A Synthesis of the Law of Misrepresentation*, 22 MINN. L. REV. 939 (1938); Bannister and Weller, *Liability of Accountants for Negligent Failure to Discover Shortages*, 18 INS. COUNSEL J. 28 (1951); Note, *The Accountant's Liability—For What and to Whom*, 36 IOWA L. REV. 319 (1951).

[122] See Ultramares Corporation v. Touche, supra note 121; Stein v. Treger, 182 F. (2d) 696 (D.C. Cir. 1950).

[123] See Editorial, 10 CERTIFIED PUBLIC ACCOUNTANT 228, 229 (1930), cited Note, 31 COL. L. REV. 858, 869, n.75 (1931); PROSSER, TORTS 743; REST., TORTS Sec. 552, comments (g), (h) (1938).

[124] 33 Cal. (2d) 80, 199 P. (2d) 1 (1948).

[125] See Comments, 37 GEO. L. J. 627 (1949); 2 VAND. L. REV. 495 (1949). But see Notes, 47 MICH. L. REV. 1232 (1949); 27 TEX. L. REV. 732 (1949).

[126] See Prosser, supra note 3, at 389; Prosser, *Joint Torts and Several Liability*, 25 CALIF. L. REV. 413, 420, 432 et seq. (1937).

shadowed in a decision referred to in the *Summers* case in which the same court held that, under the doctrine of res ipsa,[127] "where a plaintiff receives unusual injuries while unconscious and in the course of medical treatment, all those defendants who had any control over his body or the instrumentalities which might have caused the injuries may properly be called upon to meet the inference of negligence by giving an explanation of their conduct."[128] These and other cases discussed in the preceding sections will be reëxamined below in the light of the theory of liability for negligence without fault here proposed as the "true rule" of the negligence liability of dangerous enterprise.

---

[127] See supra, § 4.

[128] Ybarra v. Spangard, 25 Cal. (2d) 486, 494, 154 P. (2d) 687, 691 (1944). See also Cavero v. Franklin General Hospital,—Cal. (2d)—, 223 P. (2d) 471 (1950); Prosser, *Res Ipsa Loquitur in California*, supra note 59 at 223.

THE CRISIS OF THE RULE

§ 9.   I. "NEGLIGENCE" RESTATED

This study has undertaken to ascertain and analyze those types of enterprise liability which, while developed as liabilities for negligence, resemble liabilities without fault in extending, on the one hand, to harm caused by nonreprehensible conduct and, on the other hand, to harm not foreseeable by the person causing it. For the purposes of this investigation, it seems desirable to restate, disregarding many exceptions and modifications, the essential elements and functions of what is now indiscriminately referred to as liability for negligence.

Section 282 of the Restatement of Torts defines negligence as conduct "which falls below the standard established by law for the protection of others against unreasonably great risk of harm." Such conduct is seen as based either on a reprehensible state of mind[129] or on the absence of "due care"[130] measured by certain external standards. At the

---

[129] 1 AUSTIN, LECTURES ON JURISPRUDENCE (3d ed., 1869) 438; HOLLAND, THE ELEMENTS OF JURISPRUDENCE (4th ed., 1888) 94; SALMOND, TORTS (8th ed., 1936) 34; BIGELOW, TORTS (8th ed., 1907) 67 et seq. For an analysis of this theory see Edgerton, *Negligence, Inadvertence, and Indifference: The Relation of Mental States to Negligence*, 39 HARV. L. REV. 849, 850, 867 (1926).

[130] See Terry, *Negligence*, 29 HARV. L. REV. 40 (1915); Buckland, *The Duty to Take Care*, 51 L. Q. REV. 637 (1935); Green, *The Palsgraf Case*, 30 COL. L. REV. 789, 791 (1930); STREET, op. cit. supra note 12, 93 ff.; Edgerton, supra note 129, 852; Brereton, *The Duty of Care*, 14 AUST. L. J. 242 (1940); Carpenter, *Proximate Cause*, 14 SO. CALIF. L. REV. 1, 115, 416; 15 SO. CALIF. L. REV. 187, 304, 427; 16 SO. CALIF. L. REV. 1, 61 (1940-1943); Winfield, *Duty in Tortious Negligence*, 34 COL. L. REV. 41 (1934); Marceau, supra note 42, 501 n.10. The concept seems to go back to 2 BRACTON, DE LEGIBUS

first glance these definitions would seem to permit an "absolute" characterization of conduct as negligent without regard to its consequences. Since, however, proof of damage is an essential requirement of any action in negligence,[131] and since the conduct concept itself is necessarily relational in several respects,[132] an examination of the law of negligence liability can, I believe, forego a concept of negligent conduct and limit itself to one of negligent causation.

Liability for negligent causation would have to be based on a subjective conception of personal fault if the admonition of the tortfeasor were the prevailing purpose of that liability. However, the law's desire to compensate the victim without regard to personal fault has caused the courts to adopt the *objective* standard of the reasonable man.[133] Deepseated psychological reasons, yet unexplored, probably account for the fact that the law has chosen this "tour de force,"[134] phrasing a prevailingly compensatory liability in

---

ANGLIAE (Twiss ed., 1879) c. IV sec. 2, pp. 277, 278, and was reintroduced by HALE, PLEAS OF THE CROWN (1778) 472. See Moreland, supra note 16, 2 n.14, 5. Cf. Lawson, *The Duty of Care in Negligence: A Comparative Study*, 22 TUL. L. REV. 111 (1947).

[131] PROSSER, TORTS 177.

[132] My "voluntary muscular contraction" (HOLMES, op. cit. supra note 13, 91) in walking in the street outside the limits of the pedestrians' zone is identifiable as "conduct" in various relations: as exercise in the open air (as, e.g., golf), as loafing during office hours (as, e.g., horseplay), or as unlawful use of the street. The necessity of this relation becomes particularly obvious in the case of tortious omissions. Out of the boundless literature on this subject see, e.g., Edgerton, supra note 129, 852; Terry, supra note 130, *passim;* Wilson, *Some Thoughts about Negligence*, 2 OKLA. L. REV. 275, 281 (1949).

[133] This standard is "external." The Germanic, 196 U. S. 589, 25 Sup. Ct. 317 (1905). See Edgerton, supra note 129, 849; PROSSER, TORTS 224. Conceptually, the distinction between "subjective" and "objective" standards of negligence is merely one of degree. All negligent (as opposed to intentional) causation, is causation "by mistake" as judged from the standpoint of an "objective" (fictitious) observer. For a general analysis see the present writer's MISTAKE AND UNLAWFULNESS (IRRTUM UND RECHTSWIDRIGKEIT) (1931). But cf. Whittier, *Mistake in the Law of Torts*, 15 HARV. L. REV. 335 (1902).

[134] ROBINSON, LAW AND THE LAWYER 86 (1935). Perhaps, even strict liability was originally understood as a liability for intention,

language implying blame of a "wrongdoer's" conduct ("you should have acted as a reasonable man") rather than as an expression of the compensatory rationale of risk distribution. How the reasonable man would have acted depends on whether or not he would have foreseen that harm would ensue from his action.[135] The injunction "you shall pay for harm you expected to result from your conduct" lost much of its character as a censure when it was changed into "you shall pay for harm a reasonable man would have expected to result from your conduct." But it has lost that character almost entirely since it has come to read "you shall pay for harm caused by conduct which a reasonable man would have expected to cause some harm."[136]

Foreseeability of harm by the reasonable man does not render the actor liable if he was unable to avoid the causative conduct,[137] or if his conduct was lawful or "excused" because he could not be "reasonably" expected to avoid it,

---

conscious or subconscious. See STREET, op. cit. supra note 12, and supra § 2.

[135] "The whole idea of risk . . . is comprehended in the notion of foresight . . ." Harper, *The Foreseeability Factor in the Law of Torts*, 7 NOTRE DAME LAWYER 468 (1932). For a short bibliography and a discussion of the problem along the lines of the present investigation, see Gregory, *Proximate Cause in Negligence—A Retreat from "Rationalization,"* 6 U. of CHI. L. REV. 36 (1938). See also *Loss-Shifting*, supra note 1, 729 et seq.; Morris, *On the Teaching of Legal Cause* 39 COL. L. REV. 1087 (1939); Updegraff, *A Technique for Determining Legal Liability Based on Negligence*, 27 IOWA L. REV. 2 (1941); Malone, *Theories of Causation in the Law of Negligence*, 11 Kans. B. J. 353 (1943); Note, *Impact of the Risk Theory on the Law of Negligence*, 63 HARV. L. REV. 671 (1950); James, *The Qualities of the Reasonable Man in Negligence Cases*, 16 MO. L. REV. 1 (1951); James, *Proof of the Breach in Negligence Cases (Including Res Ipsa Loquitur)*, 37 VA. L. REV. 179 (1951).

[136] See WHARTON, A TREATISE ON THE LAW OF NEGLIGENCE 12 (1st ed., 1874). Cardozo's doctrine of the "unforeseeable plaintiff" (PROSSER, TORTS 182), as well as its modification in the "unforeseeable class" theory [Sinram v. Pennsylvania R. Co., 61 F. (2d) 767 (C.C.A. 2d, 1932), REST., TORTS § 281 (b), Comment (1934)] attempt to strike a middle line between a "some harm" and a "this harm" theory. For criticism see *Loss-Shifting*, supra note 1, 731 and Judge Learned Hand in The Glendola, 47 F. (2d) 206, 207 (C.C.A. 2d, 1931).

[137] ". . . the defendant must have had at least a fair chance of avoiding

or in other words because the risk was justifiably incurred rather than "unreasonably."[138] All or some of these elements are often stated in terms of "duty of care" or "proximate causation." That those tests add nothing to the above analysis has too often been proved to require further discussion.[139]

For the purpose of this investigation negligent causation may thus be assumed where a reasonable man in the actor's place could have foreseen a harm of the type caused and (because his conduct was neither unavoidable nor justified, that is, not in violation of "due care") could have been reasonably expected to avoid such causation.

2. THE "SIAMESE-TWIN FUNCTIONS" OF ENTERPRISE LIABILITY FOR NEGLIGENCE

§ 10.   a. *Tort law.* Though by its terms implying blame for "neglectful" conduct, the negligence rule has come to be used largely to impose liability for harm caused by the lawful activities of modern enterprise. However, the original admonitory meaning and rationale of this rule, though almost forgotten, have been preserved in the language and in occasional applications of the law. The resulting conflict between the "Siamese-twin functions" of tort law, while no doubt

the infliction of harm before he becomes answerable for such a consequence of his conduct." HOLMES, op. cit. supra note 13, 163.

[138] RESTATEMENT, TORTS § 282 (1934). The cases are well classified by Terry, supra note 130, at 42, according to certain relations between the "magnitude," "utility," and "necessity" of the risks involved or to the respective values of the "collateral" and "principal" objects of protection.

[139] See the concurring opinion by Justice Traynor in Mosley v. Arden Farms Co., 26 Cal. (2d) 213, 220, 222, 157 P. (2d) 372, 376 (1945), commenting on the reasonable expectation "that in time the courts will dispel the mists that have settled on the doctrine of proximate cause in the field of negligence." And see BALLANTINE, PROBLEMS IN LAW 1248 (3d ed. 1949) on the jury instructions on proximate causation which "are usually as blind, irrational and unintelligible as incantations of an Indian medicine man in driving out the evil spirits, and less useful." For an exhaustive analysis of the problem and a selective bibliography see Prosser, supra note 3, at 369.

the basis of many a sound compromise, has produced a certain "mutual hampering effect" on both functions.[140] Admonitory considerations would seem to underlie the employer-entrepreneur's defenses of the unforeseeability of the harm caused, of an intervening act of an independent contractor, and of plaintiff's contributory negligence.[141] Similar considerations would seem to explain why the employer-entrepreneur can be held liable for punitive damages,[142] why he is denied recourse against other tortfeasors[143] ("the law does not help the wrongdoer"), and why, notwithstanding the intervention of an independent contractor, he may be held for the violation of a "nondelegable" duty.[144]

---

[140] Morris, *Rough Justice and Some Utopian Ideas*, 24 ILL. L. REV. 730, 733 (1930). See also ibid: "The attempt is to compensate the plaintiff for one set of reasons, and to punish the defendant for an entirely different set of reasons, by the single act of making the defendant pay a sum of money to the plaintiff."

[141] See, e.g., Cooley, *Problems in Contributory Negligence*, 89 U. of PA. L. REV. 335 (1941); Paton, *Contributory Negligence—Report of the Law Revision Committee*, 14 AUST. L. J. 379 (1941); James, supra note 12, 395. This entire phase of the problem including "comparative negligence," "last clear chance," and "assumption of risk," will be discussed separately.

[142] See, e.g., Goddard v. Grand Trunk R.R. of Canada, 57 Me. 202 (1862); New Orleans, etc. R.R. v. Bailey, 40 Miss. 395 (1866); Holmes, *Agency*, 4 HARV. L. REV. 345 (1891). For a fine Comment on the *"Insurer's Liability for Punitive Damages,"* see 14 MO. L. REV. 175 (1949).

[143] See GREGORY, LEGISLATIVE LOSS DISTRIBUTION IN NEGLIGENCE ACTIONS (1936); Gregory, *Contribution Among Joint Tortfeasors: A Defense*, 54 HARV. L. REV. 1170 (1941); Bohlen, *Contribution and Indemnity between Tortfeasors*, 21 CORN. L. Q. 552 (1936); Leflar, *Contribution and Indemnity between Tortfeasors*, 81 U. of PA. L. REV. 130 (1932); James, *Contribution Among Joint Tortfeasors: A Pragmatic Criticism*, 54 HARV. L. REV. 1156 (1941); Kinnally, *Contribution or Indemnity Among Joint Tortfeasors*, 18 NOTRE DAME LAWYER 36 (1942); Notes, *Legislative Efforts to Distribute Loss Between Joint Tortfeasors*, 45 HARV. L. REV. 369 (1931); *Indemnity and Contribution Between Joint Tortfeasors*, 34 YALE L. J. 427 (1925); 21 MINN. L. REV. 764 (1937). See also N. Y. State Leg. Doc. (1941) No. 65 (A), *Report of the Law Revision Commission* (1941) 29 et seq., with references to earlier studies; and Meriam and Thornton, *Indemnity between Tort-Feasors: An Evolving Doctrine in the New York Court of Appeals*, 25 N.Y.U.L. REV. 845, 858 (1950).

[144] See, e.g., Notes, 49 W. VA. L. Q. 59 (1942); 87 U. of PA. L. REV.

On the other hand, it should be admitted "in all honesty ... that there are now large areas of employer responsibility [to third persons], which cannot be accounted for realistically" upon a rationalization based on either the employer's or the employee's fault.[145] The employer's failure carefully to select and control his employee, though perhaps the original basis of his liability,[146] cannot be relied on, since neither careful selection nor careful control can be pleaded as a defense.[147] And the employee's fault is hardly enough since few employees would be held personally liable on such slender evidence of "negligence" as a jury might deem sufficient to impose liability on their wealthy and presumably insured employers. Indeed, verdicts against employers have occasionally been upheld though based on the very negligence of which their employees had been acquitted.[148] Whether these and other anomalies can be ra-

---

728; authorities collected in STEFFEN, CASES ON THE LAW OF AGENCY, 247 et seq. (1933).

[145] Steffen, *Independent Contractor and the Good Life*, supra note 58, at 507.

[146] See, e.g., Sleath v. Wilson, 9 Car. & P. 607, 611, 173 Eng. Rep. 976, 978 (1839): "This is for the purpose of inducing those who employ others that they employ proper persons"; Goddard v. Grand Trunk Ry. of Canada, supra note 142. See also Seavey, supra note 24, 447. This theory "need not be taken seriously." Radin, supra note 12, 707.

[147] See Y. B. Smith, supra note 24, 455, 724; Steffen, supra note 58, Douglas, *Vicarious Liability and Administration of Risk*, 38 YALE L. J. 584, 720 (1929). This is true even under a statute providing for such a plea. See Miller, *The Master-Servant Concept and Judge-Made Law*, 1 LOYOLA L. REV. 25, 30 (1941): Section 2320 of the Louisiana Civil Code which declares an employer to be liable only where he might have prevented the servant's act, has been construed out of the text. Legal historians and sociologists now have occasion to observe a similar development of a respondeat superior rule from a device of admonition into one of compensation. The Supreme Court of Austria, interpreting a statute clearly based on an admonitory rationale (Austrian Civil Code, Sec. 1315), has recently declared that strict liability analogies must be applied in determining the enterprise master's liability for his servant. See supra note 52.

[148] See infra § 19. Even where the employee's fault demands punishment, threat of discharge and criminal prosecution will prove more effective than an uncollectible judgment. Similar considerations underlie

tionalized under a new theory of enterprise liability will be
discussed below.

§ 11.   b. *Insurance*. Notwithstanding judicial, legislative,
and contractual extensions of vicarious liability,[149] even an
admittedly compensatory law of enterprise liability could
not fully secure indemnification unless supported by some
scheme insuring the solvency of the party liable. Where
"self-insurance" is not feasible because of the peculiarity of
the risk or the size of the enterprise, liability insurance has
come to supplement and correct the law of torts. The consequences of this development have been manifold and
significant. On the one hand, liability insurance has not es-
caped the conflict between admonitory and compensatory
policies inherent in the liability insured. On the other hand,
the very existence of liability insurance has greatly affected
the development of that conflict.

Only in exceptional situations can an adequate distribution of risk be expected through the victim's own insurance
of his property, accident, or life. The member of the public
who in a single day may be a railroad passenger, an automobile guest, a consumer of food, and a hospital patient,
cannot be expected to carry insurance against all risks thus
incurred. Yet, where such insurance can be expected, as in
the case of the house owner and his fire risk, tort law has
been significantly affected by the availability of insurance.
Once "negligence" is established in the setting of fire, mere
physical remoteness of the damaged property will not limit
the defendant's liability. In the balance of equities the innocent victim's claim to compensation weighs more heavily
than any injustice done to the defendant by the imposition
of a burden out of proportion to his fault.[150] But this proportion may be decisive where the victim could and should
have secured insurance protection. Thus, in the largely

---

those Continental automobile statutes which exempt the professional
chauffeur from their (strict) liability rule.

[149] See James, supra note 12, 564 et seq.
[150] See PROSSER, TORTS 346.

metropolitan jurisdiction of New York availability and generality of such insurance has produced a unique limitation of the liability for negligent fires to the next adjoining house.[151] Similar developments have occurred, and are likely to occur, with regard to liability insurance.[152]

For the last fifty years that insurance, by protecting the injurer-entrepreneur, has removed many obstacles against the expansion of his liability for harm inflicted by lawful activities.[153] Similarly, the existence, or even availability, of liability insurance has rendered irrelevant, and occasionally overcome, the rationale of other immunities, such as those of members of the plaintiff's family (protection of the integrity of the family)[154] or of infants (humanitarian reasons).[155] And, overtaking legal progress by great strides, insurance business has begun to protect victims of dangerous activities without regard to the injurer's liability.

Once the impact of liability insurance on liability is recognized as legitimate, evidence of the existence of such insurance must become generally admissible.[156] And ultimately the victim will secure his compensation by direct suit against the insurer, now only occasionally permitted where the injurer is unascertainable, absent, or insolvent.

Insurance protection of the public against the hazards of modern enterprise, however greatly expanded judicially, legislatively, and contractually, can be complete only under some system of compulsion. In the fields of workmen's com-

---

[151] See Ryan v. New York Cent. R.R., 35 N. Y. 210, 91 Am. Dec. 49 (1866); Note, 32 COL. L. REV. 911 (1932).

[152] *Assurance Oblige,* supra note 1, at 450 with references.

[153] See McNeely, *The Genealogy of Liability Insurance Law,* 7 U. of PITT. L. REV. 169 (1941); Headley, *The Growth and History of Automobile Insurance* in 1 HOWE, READINGS ON INSURANCE (1923); MICHEL, ESSAY D'UNE THÉORIE GÉNÉRALE SUR L'ASSURANCE-RESPONSABILITÉ (1914).

[154] See James, supra note 9, 553; McCurdy, *Torts between Persons in Domestic Relations,* 43 HARV. L. REV. 1030 (1930); and supra note 99.

[155] See James, supra note 9, 554 with references.

[156] See Note, *Disclosure of Insurer's Interest in Voir Dire Examination of Jurors in Illinois,* 43 ILL. L. REV. 650 (1948); J. R. Wilson, *Evidence of Insurance Liability in Texas,* 2 BAYLOR L. REV. 25 (1949).

pensation[157] and automobile insurance[158] recognition of this fact has produced legislative schemes which are being advocated also for other types of enterprise liability.[159]

This entire development is greatly hampered by the lack of a distinction between the admonitory and compensatory elements of "negligence" liability. Affecting the entire field of that liability, insurance has come to protect the guilty with the innocent, thus defeating whatever remains of the original rationale of liability for moral negligence. This fact may partly account for the historical and still persisting doubt as to the "legality" of liability insurance in general,[160] a doubt which, I believe, would become meaningless in relation to the "true rule" of enterprise liability.

---

[157] See PROSSER, TORTS 518 et seq.; and e.g., J. Smith, *Sequel to Workmen's Compensation Acts*, 27 HARV. L. REV. 344 (1914); Lenhoff, *Insurance Features of Workmen's Compensation Laws*, 29 CORN. L. Q. 176, 353 (1943, 1944).

[158] See, e.g., Note, *Auto-Accidents—What Shall We Do About Them?*, 27 MINN. L. REV. 103 (1942); supra note 8.

[159] See, e.g., with regard to products liability, Jeanblanc, *Manufacturers' Liability to Persons Other Than Their Immediate Vendees*, 24 VA. L. REV. 134 (1937); with regard to railroad liability, Ballantine, *A Compensation Plan for Railway Accident Claims*, supra note 44.

[160] See McNeely, *Illegality as a Factor in Liability Insurance*, 41 COL. L. REV. 26 (1941); Gardner, *Insurance against Tort Liability—An Approach to the Cosmology of Law*, 15 LAW AND CONTEMP. PROB. 454, 462 (1950).

Part Two

THE TRUE RULE: "NEGLIGENCE WITHOUT FAULT"

"Who hews too close must miss the mark;
 truth too much truth is dying truth.
 Obiter glows in gathering dark, colors
 the clouds of doom with youth."

Llewellyn, *Put in His Thumb* 3 (1931)

THE NEW RATIONALE

§ 12.   What has been shown so far is that, when the industrial revolution demanded a new rule to protect the victims of the hazards of modern mechanical enterprise, various historical, economic, and psychological reasons prompted the courts to grope for this new rule within the traditional law of negligence (§§ 2, 3). It has further been shown that this technique ignored the inapplicability to harm of a type inevitably caused by lawful activities, of a liability for the reprehensible causation of avoidable harm (§§ 4, 9); that consequently, to make the old rule serve new needs, legalistic devices had to be used, such as the doctrines of res ipsa loquitur (presumption of or prima facie case for reprehensible conduct) and respondeat superior (imputation of such conduct to lawful enterprise) (§ 4); and that this development can be observed in many fields of enterprise liability (some of which have been specifically discussed, §§ 5-8). After a restatement of the concept of negligence (§ 9) it has finally been suggested that the use of that concept which implies blame, within a scheme of liability primarily designed to secure compensation, has caused many inconsistencies (§§ 10, 11).

In the following pages the attempt will be made to show that some of these inconsistencies can perhaps be removed by a conscious analysis of what may be characterized as a law of liability for "negligence without fault," gradually and nonconsciously developed within the traditional concept of fault. In a search for the rationale and scope of that liability it seems appropriate first to examine those enterprise liabilities which, as "strict" liabilities, developed their language and rationale independently from the law of negligence.

I. STRICT AND QUASI-STRICT ENTERPRISE LIABILITIES

§ 13.   a. At different times, in different countries, under the civil as well as under the common law, a *"strict"* or "absolute" liability[1] has been connected with certain activities.[2] The similarity of these "strict liability" rules under the several legal systems can hardly be coincidence. This similarity should keep us from belittling such rules in our own law as relics of a by-gone age,[3] and it certainly justifies the search for a common rationale.

This search is hampered by the fact that these liabilities, even after the decline of the writ system, have never been organized under a general principle, and thus could not withstand the intrusion of the fault dogma into their language, if not their substance.[4] Thus the doctrine of respondeat superior was rationalized as a liability for fault,[5] even after having been divested of the meaningless fiction

---

[1] The term "strict liability" now seems to be generally preferred. While J. Smith still speaks of "*Tort and Absolute Liability*," 30 HARV. L. REV. 241 (1917), and Winfield still finds it necessary to plead for "strict" liability as the better term [*The Myth of Absolute Liability*, 42 L. Q. REV. 37 (1926)], the leading textbooks by HARPER, A TREATISE ON THE LAW OF TORTS (1933) and PROSSER, HANDBOOK OF THE LAW OF TORTS (1941) now use "strict liability" almost exclusively.

[2] See PROSSER, TORTS 426 ff.; HARPER, op. cit. supra note 1, 331 ff.; James, *Accident Liability: Some Wartime Developments*, 55 YALE L. J. 365 (1946); Takayanagi, *Liability without Fault in the Modern Civil and Common Law*, 16 ILL. L. REV. 163, 268; 17 ILL. L. REV. 187, 416 (1921-1923). For a survey of the Continental literature on liability without fault see BIENENFELD, LIABILITIES WITHOUT FAULT (Haftungen ohne Verschulden) (1933). See also the writer's TORT LIABILITY FOR FAULT (Schuldhaftung im Schadenersatzrecht) 40 (1936).

[3] See J. Smith, *Tort and Absolute Liability—Suggested Changes in Classification*, 30 HARV. L. REV. 241, 319, 409 (1916-1917).

[4] See Part I, §§ 2 et seq. On the change incurred by the action for trespass to land under this impact see Winfield and Goodhart, *Trespass and Negligence*, 49 L. Q. REV. 358, 363 (1933); James, supra note 2, 366; and RESTATEMENT, TORTS § 166 (1934).

[5] See Part I, § 3.

identifying the master with the guilty employee.[6] The same is true, to a varying degree, for the liability for animals, for the rule of *Rylands v. Fletcher*, and for the liability for fire caused by railroad sparks.[7] And even the liability for blasting has been said to be "actually based on fault—a very high degree of fault verging on that characterized as intentionality."[8] This as well as the opposite tendency transforming the fault concept into a tool of strict liability, has obscured the rationale of the historical strict liabilities, and, to some extent, justified the statement that the question whether there is "liability with or without 'fault' must beg its own conclusion."[9] But it is submitted that *the scope of these strict liabilities can perhaps furnish the clue to their rationale* and, in further analysis, to that of the "true rule" of the related enterprise liability for "negligence."

Under an ancient rule the owner of a wild animal is "strictly" liable for harm caused by it. Does this liability extend to harm caused by a tiger who was released from its

---

[6] Holmes, *Agency*, 4 HARV. L. REV. 345 (1891); Seavey, *Speculations as to "Respondeat Superior,"* HARVARD LEGAL ESSAYS 445 et seq. (1934); Radin, *A Speculative Inquiry into the Nature of Torts*, 21 TEX. L. REV. 697, 707 (1943). For a novel "status" theory see Miller, *The Master-Servant Concept and Judge-Made Law*, 1 LOYOLA L. REV. 25 (1941).

[7] See HOLMES, THE COMMON LAW 20, 156 (1881); 1 STREET, THE FOUNDATIONS OF LEGAL LIABILITY 51, 62 ff. (1906); PRIBOY, L'IDÉE DE FAUTE ET LA RESPONSABILITÉ DES CHOSES INANIMÉES (1914); VITRY, LA DETERMINATION DU FAIT DE L'HOMME, DU FAIT DE L'ANIMAL ET DU FAIT DE LA CHOSE (1932) (animals); Harper, *Liability without Fault and Proximate Cause*, 30 MICH. L. REV. 1002, 1005 (1932); J. Smith, supra note 3, at 414, n.23; Dickinson, *The Law Behind Law:* II, 29 COL. L. REV. 285, 287 (1929); Molloy, *Fletcher v. Rylands, A Reexamination of Juristic Origins*, 9 U. OF CHI. L. REV. 266, 268, n.13 (1942); [Rylands rule; on the relation between the Rylands and the nuisance doctrines see Paton, *Liability for Nuisance*, 37 ILL. L. REV. 1 (1942); Radin, supra note 6, 711]; Note, *Absolute Liability for Negligence*, 17 NOTRE DAME LAWYER 70 (1941) (railroads).

[8] Cooley, *Problems in Contributory Negligence*, 89 U. of PA. L. Rev. 335, 351 (1941). But cf. HARPER, op. cit. supra note 1, 407. For a "moral" rationalization of workmen's compensation see Radin, supra note 6, 709.

[9] PROSSER, TORTS 431.

chain by lightning? Though Lord Bramwell once thought it did,[10] the law is clearly to the contrary. The owner leading along a street a docile bear is not liable for injuries caused by a horse frightened by the bear's appearance.[11] Limitations concerning the manner of occurrence and the scope of protected parties,[12] have in general been based on the consideration that the harm caused was not "within the extraordinary risk whose existence calls for such [strict] responsibility."[13]

If negligent causation is causation of foreseeable and avoidable harm, harm caused by the keeping of a wild animal is negligently caused. But, having been permitted or even encouraged by the law, the defendant's conduct lacks the reprehensibility required for the imposition of liability for negligence. In some cases strict liability is the price an entrepreneur must pay for that permission. Under the above rule that liability extends to all harm for the infliction of which he would be liable but for the permission, i.e. to that "general type of harm" the causation of which was foreseeable and avoidable when he started his hazardous activity, no less—no more.[14] This *"typicality"* test, unlike the general "foreseeability" test of fault liability, delimits the liability for hazardous lawful activities as "one of the necessary burdens and expenses incident to such activities."[15]

§ 14.　　b. With its liability for *"ultrahazardous activities,"* the American Law Institute has taken a further and, potentially at least, decisive step towards the recognition of a new rationale of enterprise liability. Courageously abandoning the language of the traditional strict liabilities (where

---

[10] Nichols v. Marsland (1875) L. R. 10 Ex. 255, 260.

[11] Bostock-Ferari Amusement Co. v. Brocksmith, 34 Ind. App. 566, 73 N.E. 281 (1905). See also Scribner v. Kelley, 38 Barb. 14 (N. Y. 1862); PROSSER, TORTS 458.

[12] Robinson v. Kilvert, 41 Ch. Div. 88, 94 (1889).

[13] PROSSER, TORTS 458.

[14] See HARPER, op. cit. supra note 1, 365. See also id. at 357, 392, 401.

[15] Id. at 351.

there is still much talk of presumptions of negligence or violations of duty), Section 519 of the Restatement advocates a new liability for foreseeable, though unavoidable, consequences of lawful, though hazardous, conduct. Under that provision:

> one who carries on an ultrahazardous activity is liable to another whose person, land or chattels the actor should *recognize as likely to be harmed* by the unpreventable miscarriage of the activity for harm resulting thereto from that which makes the activity ultrahazardous, although the *utmost care* is exercised to prevent the harm. (Italics mine.)

This rule would admirably fit all kinds of mechanical enterprise if it could be applied to every ultrahazardous activity, defined in Section 520 as one which "necessarily involves a risk of serious harm to the person, land or chattels of others which cannot be eliminated by the exercise of the utmost care." Under this formula a railroad would be liable for fire caused in a distant cottage by a spark from its engine.[16] For, harm of this type was "likely" to result from this "unpreventable miscarriage" of its activity. On the other hand, the railroad would not be liable for the death of children drowned when chasing a kite across a frozen pond formed through the railroad's negligence.[17] For, those facts which make a railroad's activity "ultrahazardous" (such as speed or emission of sparks) did not cause the children's death.

This rule, while not adopted by the courts,[18] seems to express the missing rationale of the "negligence" liability of

---

[16] See infra note 39. No doubt there would be some limit to that distance which would be for the jury to determine.

[17] See Part I, note 2.

[18] Apparently the first case to impose liability under the Restatement doctrine where strict liability would not have been imposed previously, is Luthringer v. Moore, 31 Cal. (2d) 489, 190 P. (2d) 1 (1948). A fumigator was held liable for personal injuries caused by the escape of hydrocyanic acid gas. While talking extensively in terms of the Restatement, the case seems inconclusive in view of its ultimate reliance on the pre-Restatement case of Green v. General Petroleum Corp. 205 Cal. 328, 270 Pac. 952 (1928). Equally doubtful is the scope of Chapman Chemi-

mechanical enterprise for unpreventable calculable harm. But Section 520 expressly excludes from the liability under Section 519 all activities which are a "matter of common usage." The scope of this exception is obscure. Oilwells are covered because "the dangers incident thereto are characteristic of oil lands and not of lands in general."[19] On the other hand, railroads, and thus probably the very enterprise risks here discussed, are excluded as "of common usage" and, therefore, within the generally recognized domain of the negligence rule. Yet, in our search for a rationale of enterprise liability for negligence, the Restatement rule remains a significant attempt at formulating dormant thought.

§ 15.   c. Strict tort liabilities have proved to be limited to harm typically and calculably caused by a dangerous activity, and the Restatement liability for "ultrahazardous activities" is similarly determined. A further clue to the rationale of those liabilities can perhaps be gained by examining the liability for *breach of contract* which can be, and often has been, invoked to obtain strict liability in the absence of a tort rule to that effect.[20] Under the classic case of *Hadley v. Baxendale*,[21] damages for breach of contract are "such as may reasonably be supposed to have been *in the contemplation of both parties, at the time they made the contract,* as the probable result of the breach of it."[22] Whether or not

---

cal Co. v. Taylor, 215 Ark. 630, 222 S. W. (2d) 820 (1949). Cf. Burns v. Vaughn, —Ark.—, 224 S. W. (2d) 365 (1949). See in general Comment, *Absolute Liability for Ultrahazardous Activities: An Appraisal of the Restatement Doctrine,* 37 CALIF. L. REV. 269 (1949).

[19] RESTATEMENT, TORTS § 520, Comment (e) (1938).

[20] Although the contract rule reduces the scope of liability with regard to "privity" and punitive damages. See 5 CORBIN ON CONTRACTS §§ 1019, 1077 (1951). See also Seavey, supra note 6, 444. Election is facilitated by the uncertainty of the line between tort and contract law. See PROSSER, TORTS 201 ff., with references.

[21] 9 Ex. 341, 156 Eng. Rep. 145 (1854). For references to more recent cases see PATTERSON-GOBLE, CASES ON CONTRACTS 829 (1941); CORBIN op. cit. supra note 20, § 1007.

[22] Italics added. Hadley v. Baxendale, supra note 21, at 354, 156 Eng. Rep. at 151.

the scope of this rule "is much narrower than the 'proximate consequence' rule which prevails in actions to recover for tort,"[23] *Hadley v. Baxendale*, by relating the foreseeability test to the time of the making of the contract, rather than to the time of its breach, has made a significant contribution to the understanding of the rationale of the entrepreneur's non-fault liability in general.

In thus limiting liability, the law, on the one hand, "manifests a policy to encourage the entrepreneur by reducing the extent of his risk,"[24] and, on the other hand, imposes on the entrepreneur liability for harm foreseeable by him as typical[25] at the time of the start of his activity whether or not that harm was foreseeable by him or by his employee at the time of the causation by that employee of the particular harm.

While the contract rule can be directly applied only in those strict liability cases where, as in *Hadley v. Baxendale* and other common carrier cases, the damaging act is construed as a breach of contract, this rule remains meaningful even where no contract relation can be established. Here, the contemplation test may be related to a hypothetical "agreement" between the entrepreneur and the state, under which the enterprise is permitted or "licensed" in spite of its known dangerous nature, in consideration of the assumption of full liability for those, and only those, damages which "may reasonably be supposed to have been in the contemplation of both parties at the time they made the contract," that is, when the "license" was granted.[26] Causation

---

[23] Patterson, *The Apportionment of Business Risks Through Legal Devices*, 24 COL. L. REV. 335, 342 (1924). This has become doubtful since Victoria Laundry (Windsor) Ld. v. Newman Industries Ld. [1949] 2 K.B. 528, 543; and Monarch S.S. Co. v. Karlshamns Oljefabriker (A/B) [1949] A.C. 196. See P.S. James, *Measure of Damages in Contract and Tort —Law and Fact*, 13 MOD. L. REV. 36 (1950); CORBIN op. cit. supra note 20, § 1019.

[24] Patterson, supra note 23, at 342. Italics omitted.

[25] See now Victoria Laundry (Windsor) Ld. v. Newman Industries Ld., supra note 23.

[26] Cf. SALMOND, JURISPRUDENCE, 456 (1922) according to whom certain activities are "tolerated only on the condition of making

of such (typical) harm could be considered as bringing this "contractual" liability into operation whether or not the harmful event was preceded by "fault."

Liability contracts of this kind between entrepreneur and society have occurred in reality. A coal company had been granted permission by the city council to use explosives, on the undertaking to make good any damage to person or property arising from its dangerous activity. In a suit claiming damage to real estate the court held for plaintiff without proof of negligence because "by going ahead, defendant assumed that obligation."[27] In another case a construction agreement between a contractor and a municipal authority, under which the contractor assumed responsibility for all damage caused by blasting, was held to create strict liability to any third party injured.[28] The contractual contemplation test to be applied in these cases in analogy to *Hadley v. Baxendale* is distinct from the traditional foreseeability test of the negligence rule and identical in result with the typicality tests of strict tort liability, and of the Restatement liability for ultrahazardous activities: *Anticipation of harm at the time of the start of the activity rather than the time of the injurious conduct determines the scope of liability.* It is this determination which reveals the rationale of the non-fault liabilities discussed: these *liabilities are the price which must be paid to society for the permission of a hazardous activity.*

---

compensation to all who suffer from it"; and Bohlen, *Fifty Years of Torts,* 50 HARV. L. REV. 725 (1937). The suggested analogy could perhaps be followed through also in another respect: Where the injurer has not obtained the prescribed license, i.e., where he has not concluded the "contract" providing for the imposition of a (strict but reduced) "enterprise" liability, his (full) liability for his "initial" negligence (in starting a dangerous enterprise) has remained in force. Such a theory would rationalize those cases, now considered anomalous, which render the driver of an unlicensed automobile liable for injuries to another traveler without regard to causal fault ("Massachusetts rule"). See e.g., Capano v. Melchionno, 297 Mass. 1, 10, 7 N. E. (2d) 593, 598 (1937), and cases in Note, 163 A. L. R. 1375, 1392 (1946).

[27] Baier v. Glen Alden Coal Co., 332 Pa. 562, 3 A. (2d) 349 (1939).

[28] Coley v. Cohen, 289 N. Y. 365, 45 N. E. (2d) 913 (1942). See also dissent by Finch, J; Phinney v. Boston Elevated R. R., 201 Mass. 286,

§ 16.   2. ENTERPRISE LIABILITIES FOR "NEGLIGENCE
         WITHOUT FAULT."

The failure of the law of strict liability to develop a common
rationale and to resist the language and rationalization of
fault liability may have been partly responsible for the fact
that the "common sense of an industrial society" had to
make its way within the law of negligence "against minds
steeped in the absolutes of a once common law."[29] However, beginnings just discussed of a new understanding of
non-fault liability should gain new force in the entire law of
enterprise liability at this time, when that other reason for
the repression of strict liability, the desire to protect the
growing industry, seems outweighed by the wealth of corporate enterprise and its ability to distribute its cost by
liability insurance and price calculation.

In fact, as has been shown,[30] the scope of the negligence
liability of enterprises not strictly liable has approached
that of a strict liability for typical causation, and the similarity between both types of liabilities as to their rationale
has become increasingly obvious: Exposing the community
to risk, rather than causation of the individual harm has
become the basis of liability in both fields,[31] even in countries in which fault has been called "the mother of all enterprise liability."[32]

The similarities between the fault and non-fault liabilities
of modern enterprise regarding their basis and rationale
justify a similar theoretical analysis. The contract analogy
seems applicable to both types of liability if a promise by

---

87 N. E. 490 (1909); Confreda v. George H. Flinn Corp., 68 N. Y. S.
(2d) 925 (Kings Co., 1947).

[29] Hamilton, *The Living Law*, 26 SURVEY GRAPHIC 632, 635 (1937).

[30] See Part I, §§ 5, 8.

[31] PROSSER, TORTS, 429. See also Seavey, *Principles of Torts*, 56
HARV. L. REV. 72, 86 (1942).

[32] CROISSANT, HAFTPFLICHT UND EIGENES VERSCHUL-
DEN, 35.

the entrepreneur is assumed to indemnify anybody "typically" injured by the enterprise; a promise made in consideration of the toleration of the "initial negligence," committed by starting the dangerous enterprise.[33] Closely akin to the contract analogy is the theory of "assumption of responsibility," proposed for the "manufacturer's" liability in Section 16-B of the Revised Second Draft of the Uniform Sales Act.[34] That calculability of the harm should be, and to some extent is, the proper test of both strict and "quasi-strict" liabilities has probably found its most striking expression where liability is made to depend upon the existence of liability insurance.[35]

Frequently railroads and automobile operators are, under the negligence rule, "really" not held for a particular "fault" occurring in their operations, but, as under rules of strict liability, for the inevitable consequences of their dangerous activities which, but for their being tolerated because of a superior interest, would be "negligent" because of being foreseeably harmful. In this sense this enterprise liability for "negligence" is "strict" in that it is imposed on lawful rather than on reprehensible conduct; and the purportedly required "negligence" in the railroad engineer's or automobile driver's incorrect reaction is reduced to a mere vehicle of a "quasi-strict" liability for dangerous enterprise.

The entrepreneur's duty to pay damages for an injury, from the inflicting of which he has "a right not to be prevented,"[36] is analogous to the results of the rule permitting but sanctioning the infliction of harm by *"necessity."* This analogy has more than dogmatic significance. In both situ-

---

[33] See SPILREIN, LE CONTRACT D'ASSURANCE DE RESPONSABILITÉ CIVILE (1934) 23: "The *guaranty* of indemnification for all damage done is the consideration for the risks imposed upon others by dangerous things" (translation, italics added).

[34] Report and Second Draft, THE REVISED UNIFORM SALES ACT (1941). Section 2—315 of the 1950 Draft of a Uniform Commercial Code has restored the conventional language. See supra Part I, note 109.

[35] See Part I, § 6.

[36] Marceau, *Reflections on the Theory of Negligence*, 5 LA. L. REV. 495, 506 (1944), using Hohfeld's terminology.

ations—to use Professor Bohlen's formulation—"it is obviously just that he whose interests are advanced by the act
should bear the cost of doing it," though "the interest of the
actor which is served by his act may, as compared with that
which is necessarily or probably invaded by it, be of such
value that he should not be punished, and that resistance
should be discouraged by imposing liability upon one who
resists."[37] Both the navigator who is permitted on grounds
of necessity to moor his vessel to a private wharf,[38] and the
railroad which is permitted an activity inevitably resulting
in the emission of sparks into private property, may not
be resisted in their lawful activities, but they must, within
the limits to be discussed presently, pay damages for any
harm so caused.

This, of course, does not mean that the railroad or the
automobile operator could or should never be held for fault.
Where the victim has proved the engineer or the driver to
have caused the injury by an act of carelessness, for instance,
by reading a newspaper instead of watching the road, negligence liability will obtain under the same rule that would

---

[37] Bohlen, *Incomplete Privilege to Inflict Intentional Invasions of Interests of
Property and Personality*, 39 HARV. L. REV. 307, 316 (1926). See also
PROSSER, TORTS 139.

[38] Vincent v. Lake Erie Transportation Co., 109 Minn. 456, 124 N. W.
221 (1910). See also Ploof v. Putnam, 81 Vt. 471, 71 Atl. 188 (1908);
Depue v. Flatau, 100 Minn. 299, 111 N. W. 1 (1907); Marceau, supra
note 36, 506; PROSSER, TORTS, 139; RESTATEMENT, TORTS
§§ 296, 470 (1934); WINFIELD, LAW OF TORT 55 (1946). In automobile cases something like a general theory of the "agony of collision"
seems to be in the making. Johnson v. Prideaux, 176 Wis. 375, 187 N. W.
207 (1922). See also HUGHES, ROAD USERS' RIGHTS, LIABILITY
AND INSURANCE, 38 (1938); 1 HARPER, READINGS IN TORTS,
320, 334 (1941). For a collection and discussion of the authorities see
Carpenter, *Proximate Cause*, 14 SO. CAL. L. REV. 1, 115, 416; 14 SO.
CAL. L. REV. 187, 304, 427; 16 SO. CAL. L. REV. 1, 61 (1940-1943);
Evans, *The Standard of Care in Emergencies*, 31 KY. L. J. 207 (1943). This
problem has been given much attention in Continental legal literature.
See the writer's MISTAKE AND UNLAWFULNESS (Irrtum und
Rechtswidrigkeit) (1931), and TORT LIABILITY FOR FAULT
(Schuldhaftung im Schadenersatzrecht) (1936) 198 ff; *Assurance Oblige*,
supra Part I, note 1, at 445 et seq.

apply to a person who carelessly fired a shot in a city street. Only that type of "negligence" consisting in a technical error, which, though often artificially construed and concluded from surrounding circumstances, usually supports present-day enterprise liability for inevitable accidents, requires, I believe, the new rationale.

The need for this rationale appears even more clearly in the courts' attempts at determining the *scope* of this enterprise liability for so-called "negligence." The "foreseeability" test as generally used has proved inapplicable. Where a railroad engineer had "negligently" run his train into a landslide which, a few minutes before (after another train had passed undamaged), had blocked the tracks, it is to mislead the jury to ask it whether the engineer "could have anticipated the burning of the plaintiff's property," several hundred feet away, by oil ignited on the train by the impact and carried to that property by an adjoining, suddenly swollen creek.[39] And it is to mislead court and jury to ask whether the foreman who inadvertently failed to keep open the culvert should have reasonably foreseen that children chasing a kite across a frozen pond formed by water from that culvert, would be drowned.[40] This is not and cannot be the issue for the railroad's liability. What the law wants to know is whether liability can be fairly imposed on the railroad in those cases because the harm was typical for its activities, and thus calculable and reasonably insurable. This typicality test is the one adopted in the law of strict liability.[41] It is the one suggested by the American Law Institute for its ultrahazardous activities[42] and it is the one that should be consciously recognized in the law of the "quasi-strict" liability of mechanical enterprise for negligence. That courts are groping for this solution is frequently

---

[39] Hoag v. Lake Shore and M.S. R. R., 85 Penn. St. 293, 27 Am. Rep. 653 (1877). While the court in this case denied liability because of lack of a "proximate cause," defendant railroad was held liable on substantially identical facts in Kuhn v. Jewett, 32 N. J. Eq. (5 Stew.) 647 (1880).

[40] See Part I, § 1.

[41] See supra § 13.

[42] See supra § 15.

apparent in their treatment of the requirements of "proximate cause" and "due care."

Where a ship and its cargo were destroyed by an explosion of petrol vapor caused by a spark emitted by a plank "negligently" dropped into the hold of the ship, the charterer's liability was not "really" based on the proximate causation or foreseeability of harm by the workman who negligently dropped the plank;[43] but, I believe, on the consideration that a charterer can calculate as typical (and can insure against) the loss by fire of a petrol cargo.

Standing on a railroad platform, Mrs. Palsgraf was injured by scales broken in a concussion caused by fireworks exploding at a considerable distance in a package which had been "negligently" dislodged from a passenger's arm by a railroad employee assisting the passenger in boarding the train. Few will quarrel with the decision denying the railroad's liability.[44] Yet, how close did Cardozo's majority opinion come to reality when he reasoned that defendant's employee could not reasonably have foreseen damage to the plaintiff?[45] And how close to this reality is Andrews in his dissent when he pleads for unlimited liability for all acts which unreasonably threaten the safety of others?[46] Was not the real test, with opposite results, consciously or nonconsciously applied by both Cardozo and Andrews, whether the plaintiff's injury was typical and thus calculable and insurable by the railroad? True, the answer in this case and in many other cases would not be easy even if the issue were so phrased. But neither juries nor judges should be misled by talk of "proximate" or "direct" cause, "due care," "duty to foreseeable plaintiffs," or "intervening forces." Only by relating the consequences to the enterprise activity itself rather than to the individual causative act, can liability be

---

[43] In re Polemis and Furness, Withy & Co., [1921] 3 K. B. 560, 575.

[44] Palsgraf v. Long Island R. R., 248 N. Y. 339, 162 N. E. 99 (1928).

[45] Palsgraf v. Long Island R. R., supra note 44, at 345, 162 N. E. at 101. Cf. the writer's Note, *Loss-Shifting*, Part I, note 1; Wilson, *Some Thoughts about Negligence*, 2 OKLA. L. REV. 275, 284 (1949).

[46] Palsgraf v. Long Island R. R., supra note 44, at 350, 162 N. E. at 101.

restricted "to the scope of the original risk created,"[47] that is, to the "negligence without fault" inherent in the conscious assumption of a risk to be created by a lawful but dangerous activity.

The close relationship in rationale and scope between "negligence" and strict enterprise liabilities does not require, however, the legislative removal from all enterprise liability of the language of negligence, "distressingly inadequate"[48] as this terminology may have proved to be. No one formula can provide for the manifold facts requiring different limitations of liability in each case. Even countries which have adopted strict liability statutes for enterprise hazards have not been able to avoid the problems of "proximate causation" or "violation of a duty of care." And the common sense of juries is probably the best judge where the law cannot give more than a vague guidance. But one thing we owe to both judges and juries: to assist, rather than to hamper them in applying their common sense. If we mean to ask the jury whether a certain harm caused by hazardous but lawful enterprise activities can be justly imputed to the entrepreneur as being reasonably calculable and insurable by him, we must not ask the jurors whether in their opinion a reasonable man in his employee's place should have avoided the causation of that harm. No longer should "the conduct of one man [be] elaborately investigated in order to determine and fix the liability of another man."[49]

Without legislation the necessary clarification can perhaps be achieved by distinguishing *within* the law of "negligence"

---

[47] PROSSER, TORTS 342. Perhaps the questions raised id. 343 n.63 as to the limits of liability of a railroad for operating a train without a proper lookout can thus be more readily answered: Collision with a cow on the tracks is clearly within the "scope of risk," in contrast to electrocution of a man ten miles away caused by the twisting of a power line. See also Prosser, *Proximate Cause in California*, 38 CALIF. L. REV. 369, 397 (1950).

[48] Green, *Are There Dependable Rules of Causation?*, 77 U. of PA. L. REV. 601, 620 (1929).

[49] Ballantine, *A Compensation Plan for Railway Accident Claims*, 29 HARV. L. REV. 708 (1916).

between a liability based on the censure of reprehensible conduct, on the one hand, and a liability for the unavoidable and insurable consequences of lawful (enterprise) activities, on the other hand. These two types of liability could be distinguished as liabilities for "moral negligence" and "negligence without fault." This distinction would stress the non-fault character of initially "negligent" but lawful dangerous activities as opposed to unlawful negligent conduct, and would make it possible to discriminate between the "foreseeability" test of a liability for moral negligence and the typicality test of a quasi-strict liability for lawful dangerous activities.

Liability for "negligence without fault" can be no more sharply defined than negligence liability as defined above;[50] but it may roughly be said to be connected with those initially dangerous activities which, while legalized because of their social value, are held to strict liability in terms of the negligence rule. This liability may be said to include injuries which, being typical for the particular enterprise, could have reasonably been foreseen (though not avoided without abandoning the enterprise) by the entrepreneur when starting his activity.[51]

---

[50] Part I, § 9.

[51] That the word "negligence" is preserved in the terminology proposed could gain particular significance where a financially irresponsible injurer turns his initial "negligence without fault" into a "moral," perhaps even criminal negligence by not keeping his "promise" to secure indemnification to the injured by insurance or otherwise. See infra note 80.

FAULT AND NON-FAULT
LIABILITY FOR NEGLIGENCE
DISTINGUISHED AND RECONCILED:
SUMMARY AND OUTLOOK

§ 17.   I. THE SCOPE OF LIABILITY

Two motorists collided, and one car was propelled into a building. Some time later when the car was removed, a stone loosened by the accident fell from the building and killed a pedestrian. The two motorists (or rather their insurers) were held liable for the pedestrian's death. The court argued that the defendants must have foreseen that the vehicle would have to be moved from the structure, that parts of that structure would fall into the highway and that a passing pedestrian might be injured.[52] In another case a motorist was injured by a defective pillar (belonging to the defendant city) against which his car had been thrown in a collision. The court held for defendant who could not have foreseen "that a car might have been struck by another car in such a way as to cause it to come in contact with the pillar and cause the pillar to fall."[53] It has been suggested above that the "foreseeability" test, which is so clearly unrealistic in these and in innumerable similar cases, becomes meaningful if related to the hazardous activity as such rather than to the causative conduct; or, in other words, if the test of individual foreseeability is replaced by a test of general

---

[52] In re Guardian Casualty Co., 253 App. Div. 360, 2 N. Y. S. (2d) 232 (1938).
[53] Leachman v. Louisville, 270 Ky. 260, 263, 109 S. W. (2d) 614, 615 (1937).

"typicality." While death of a pedestrian near the place of collision (without regard to intervening atypical occurrences) is typical of the hazards of driving automobiles, injury to a motorist running against a pillar is not typical of the enterprise risks of a municipality responsible for the maintenance of pillars. In most cases this typicality test would merely rationalize otherwise unexplainable common sense "foreseeability" decisions of judges and juries. Occasionally, however, (as will be illustrated in the next sections), if consciously applied, it might lead to more desirable results than the misleading language about the "reasonable man's" foresight.

The substitution of typicality for foreseeability would also, I believe, cure or, at least, mitigate, the present anarchy in the determination of the amount of damages for bodily injury and death claims in enterprise liability cases. That the need for reform is increasingly recognized is apparent in the insurers' practice of fixing policy maxima and standards of recovery, and in numerous attempts of commercial digests to categorize jury assessments.[54]

Full stability and clarity in the solution of this question, as in that of many other questions of arithmetical computation, could, of course, be obtained only by statutory reform which, by introducing "tariffs" of recovery, would thus return to the oldest tort law.[55] Unless and until statutory schemes of a standardized compensation for injuries typically caused by hazardous activities replace the present common law system of individual jury assessment, some progress could probably be achieved by instructions assisting, rather than misleading, juries in their difficult task. Such instructions would have to be based on the conscious distinction within the law of negligence between enterprise liability for harm calculably and inevitably caused by enterprise hazards ("negligence without fault") and what is left of a "moral"

---

[54] See, e.g., 15 FIFTH DECENNIAL DIGEST (1936-1946), Title "Damages," VII (176 pages).

[55] See, e.g., 2 POLLOCK-MAITLAND, HISTORY OF ENGLISH LAW, 525 (1895). But see also supra Part I, notes 8, 158.

negligence liability for the foreseeable consequences of reprehensible conduct. For, on the one hand, in cases of the latter type, jury assessment should continue to take into account degrees of the injurer's fault and possibly the relative financial capacities of the parties. On the other hand, consideration of the injurer's circumstances has no place in a liability for "negligence without fault."[56] With regard to that liability, in the absence of legislation, substitution of the typicality for the present foreseeability test would serve both the injured, who could expect compensation by more uniform awards, and the injurer, who could more easily calculate his liability based upon this very calculability.

§ 18. 2. THE PLAINTIFF'S CHOICE

The proposed distinction would appear in the first place in the plaintiff's pleadings and in the charge to the jury. In cases where the harm caused by a hazardous enterprise activity was both "typical" for that activity and "foreseeable" at the time of the causative conduct, the plaintiff should have the right to choose between claims based on fault or non-fault. If he can prove foreseeability he will choose the first count under which he could hope to recover full damages and need not show typicality of the harm. If he shuns the foreseeability issue he will, on the other hand, base his complaint upon a theory of negligence without fault, resigning himself to the typicality limitations of that theory.

The charge to the jury will correspond to the plaintiff's choice. Where, as would ordinarily be the case, negligence with and without fault would be alleged in the alternative, the jury would be charged somewhat as follows:

1. The defendant is liable for "morally" negligent causation of the harm:

    (a) if he is guilty of conduct which a reasonable man would

---

[56] As to the plaintiff's choice, see infra § 18.

have been expected to avoid (except for mere faulty reactions covered by instruction 2); and

(b) if he could have reasonably foreseen that harm of the type actually caused would result from such conduct.

2. The defendant is liable for "negligence without fault":

(a) if the harm was caused by an innocently negligent ("quasi-negligent") activity, i. e., an activity initially negligent but legalized because of its social value (certain activities, such as the operation of railroads or automobiles being quasi-negligent in that sense as a matter of law); and

(b) if the harm was of a kind which could have been calculated (and therefore insured against) as typical for the particular enterprise.

No doubt, this charge too would leave room for many ambiguities and errors, but no longer would the judge (though he may not himself be misled by using misleading words), mislead the jury.[57] A pedestrian is injured by a brick projected by a passing truck. A jury which denied recovery,[58] presumably because it was reluctant to find the driver negligent, might have been willing to hold for the plaintiff on a finding of negligence without fault, that is, causation of harm typical for the hazards of driving a truck. A tubercular woman claims damages for suffering caused to her by smoke that had spread to her cottage from a railroad fire. A jury which, under the court's charge, felt compelled to hold the railroad for negligence,[59] might have denied such extraor-

---

[57] Edgerton, *Negligence, Inadvertence, and Indifference: The Relation of Mental States to Negligence*, 39 HARV. L. REV. 849, 870 (1926). See in general Note, *Instructions to the Jury in Negligence Cases*, 28 KY. L. J. 469 (1940); HUGHES, THE LAW OF INSTRUCTIONS TO JURIES (1905); James, *Functions of Judge and Jury in Negligence Cases*, 58 YALE L. J. 667 (1949); Note, *Proximate Cause—Confusion of Jurors by Misleading Label*, 34 MARQ. L. REV. 204 (1951).

[58] Demjanik v. Kultau, 242 App. Div. 255, 274 N. Y. Supp. 387 (1934).

[59] Missouri Pac. R. R. v. Johnson, 198 Ark. 1134, 133 S. W. (2d) 33 (1939). By eliminating the foreseeability issue, more realistic and consistent answers could perhaps be obtained to the much litigated question as to the liability of automobile operators to onlookers of accidents for shock injury. See Seitz, *Duty and Foreseeability Factors in Fright Cases*, 23 MARQ. L. REV. 103 (1939).

dinary liability if it had been asked whether such harm was typical for the hazards caused by the operation of railroads.

3. "THIRD-PARTY TORTFEASORS"

By the toleration of its "negligent" activities, enterprise has been immunized against the rule sanctioning the avoidable causation of harm foreseeable at the start of those activities. However, under that very rule, such enterprise has been made liable in many situations through the medium of a "third-party tortfeasor," such as the employee under the doctrine of respondeat superior,[60] the operator in automobile liability,[61] the retailer in products liability,[62] or the trustee in the trust estate's liability for torts.[63] The relation of this device to the proposed theory of negligence without fault will now be examined.

§ 19.   a. *Employer and employee. Respondeat Superior.* Many theoretical and practical difficulties could probably be clarified by conceiving the entrepreneur-master's liability primarily as one for harm typically and unavoidably caused in his lawful enterprise, rather than a liability for harm avoidably and foreseeably caused by a servant's reprehensible conduct.[64] No longer would we require an apology for rejecting the master's defense that he has carefully chosen and controlled his negligent servant.[65] No longer would an independent contractor's intervening act or the plaintiff's contributory negligence[66] be either needed to relieve the employer of a liability atypical for the hazards of his enterprise, or sufficient to preclude recovery against him for harm

---

[60] See Part I, §§ 3, 10.
[61] See Part I, § 5.
[62] See Part I, § 7.
[63] See Part I, § 6.
[64] See supra § 16.
[65] See Part I, notes 146, 147.
[66] See Part I, note 141.

typically caused by those hazards. Nor would an obsolete rationale compel holding the employer for punitive damages imposed on a morally negligent employee[67] or denying the entrepreneur recourse against other "tortfeasors" "because the law does not help the wrongdoer."[68]

Moreover, the employer's liability for the negligence of employees non-suable for, or acquitted of, that very negligence, now an erratic doctrine of a small minority and hardly tenable under the prevailing theory of negligence, could become the rule without legislative interference. Two cases may illustrate these minority doctrines.[69]

Where an automobile accident had been caused by a plank placed across the road by a highway district in the course of construction work, a jury verdict against the district was upheld notwithstanding a simultaneous verdict in favor of the foreman for whose negligence the district was held.[70] The court quoted with approval from decisions of other jurisdictions substantially arguing that one cannot exonerate oneself by referring to an inconsistent decision concerning another party.[71] Other courts have admitted this

---

[67] See Part I, note 142.

[68] See Part I, note 143.

[69] See also Part I, note 148.

[70] Strickfaden v. Greencreek Highway District, 42 Ida. 738, 248 Pac. 456 (1926); cited with approval in State v. Kouni, 58 Ida. 493, 506, 76 P. (2d) 917, 922 (1938). See also Judd v. Oregon Short Line R.R., 55 Ida. 461, 44 P. (2d) 291 (1936) (verdict of $1 against employee and of $15,720 against employer-railroad); R. J. Reynolds Tobacco Co. v. Nowby, 153 F. (2d) 819, 821 (C.C.A. 9th, 1946) (discussing and applying the first two cases).

[71] Texas & P.R.R. v. Huber, (Tex. Civ. App.) 95 S. W. 508 (1906) [approved in S. H. Kress & Co. v. Hall (Tex. Civ. App.) 154 S. W. (2d) 278 (1941)]; Whitesell v. Joplin & P.R.R., 115 Kan. 53, 222 Pac. 133 (1924) [cited with approval U.S. v. Marcus, 41 F. Supp. 197, 215 (Pa, 1941)]; Ill. Centr. R.R. v. Murphy's Adm'r, 123 Ky. 787, 798, 97 S. W. 729, 732 (1906) [since overruled, see now Chesapeake & O. R.R. v. Williams' Adm'x, 300 Ky. 850, 190 S. W. (2d) 549 (1945)]. See also St. Louis & S.F.R.R. v. Sanderson, 99 Miss. 148, 54 So. 885 (1911) [cited with approval Miss. Power & Light Co. v. Smith, 169 Miss. 447, 463, 153 So. 376, 379 (1934); without disapproval in Granquist v. Crystal Springs Lumber Co., 190 Miss. 572, 584, 1 So. (2d) 216 (1941)]. Oc-

rule to be "illogical" and defended it simply on grounds of justice.[72] But occasionally the true "logical" reason underlying this practice appears in a dictum such as that of the Mississippi Supreme Court which sees the master and the servant liable "on distinct and different legal principles— the engineer, because of his personal trespass; the railroad company, because of its failure to discharge its non-delegable duty to the public regarding the custody and management of its dangerous instrumentalities."[73] Stripped of its duty language, this statement amounts to the recognition of an entrepreneur's liability for negligence without fault "distinct and different" from the employee's liability for fault. Even more significantly the Idaho court upheld a verdict assessing damages of over $1 against a railroad engineer and of over $15,000 against his employer, on the ground that, "although the jury found that the engineer was guilty of negligence, it is not at all surprising if they concluded that, since what he was doing was for the master and *could not profit him in any way* beyond his wages, it would be *only fair for his employer to pay* whatever damages had resulted from the negligent acts committed."[74]

Another minority doctrine exemplifying the occasional recognition of an independent rationale of the employer's liability, is that expressed in a decision of the New York Court of Appeals in which a woman was permitted to recover against her husband's employer for injuries negligently inflicted on her by her husband within the scope of his employment, although under New York law she could not have

casionally courts have relied on the fact that neither the pleading nor the evidence had been limited to one particular employee. See Elgin v. Kroger Grocery & Baking Co., 357 Mo. 19, 206 S. W. (2d) 501 (1947) with additional references.

[72] See De Sandro v. Missoula Light & Water Co., 48 Mont. 226, 136 Pac. 711 (1913), stating that the plaintiff should not be deprived of his right of recovery on purely technical grounds. But cf. Lowney v. Butte El. Co., 61 Mont. 497, 204 Pac. 435 (1922).

[73] Ill. Centr. R. R. v. Clarke, 65 Miss. 691, 697, 38 So. 97, 98 (1905). See supra note 71.

[74] Judd v. Oregon Short Line R.R., supra note 70, at 58 Ida. 478, 44 P. (2d) 298. Italics added. See supra note 70.

maintained an action against her husband.[75] Under the prevailing analysis this holding can hardly be defended against the reasoning advanced in decisions to the contrary, that where the agent is not liable the principal cannot be held, since if he were so held, the agent's immunity would indirectly be destroyed by the principal's recovery over against the agent.[76] But if respondeat superior is no longer interpreted as merely transferring to the master a servant's liability for the reprehensible causation of foreseeable harm, but recognized as creating in the master an independent liability for harm typically caused within his lawful enterprise, the master's liability in such cases is easily justified. He will be held for calculable harm without regard to the occurrence of reprehensible conduct. Where the master's liability is based on a mere inadvertence of his servant, an attempt by the master to recover from his servant will hardly be successful. And where the latter has been guilty of reprehensible conduct his obligation to indemnify the master can be explained by the "breach of an independent duty."[77]

Not always is it expedient to distribute enterprise losses through the employer, as where the agent rather than the master is the entrepreneur best able to foresee and calculate losses typically and inevitably caused by his activity. This is particularly true where the agent serves several masters rather than one. To rationalize in such cases the denial of the entrepreneur's liability, courts have developed the rule of the *"independent contractor"* for whose actions the master is not liable. The difficulties in the application of this rule have proved unsurmountable notwithstanding many attempts to save it by additional artificial theories.[78]

---

[75] Schubert v. Schubert Wagon Co., 249 N. Y. 253, 164 N.E. 42 (1928).

[76] See Riegger v. Bruton Brewing Co., 178 Md. 518, 16 A. (2d) 99 (1940).

[77] See Schubert v. Schubert Wagon Co., supra note 75 at 257, 164 N. E. at 43. See also PROSSER, TORTS 909. See also Smith v. Foran, 43 Conn. 244, 21 Am. Rep. 647 (1875); Note, 26 MINN. L. REV. 730, 731 (1942).

[78] Concerning the theories of "control and selection" and of "implied authority" see e.g. Douglas, *Vicarious Liability and Administration of Risk,*

Professor Seavey assumes that the law is moving towards the abolition of the independent contractor.[79] Indeed, the entrepreneur's "control" of his agent's activity should determine the distribution of the loss only if to increase the effectiveness of such control were the primary purpose of the doctrine. While this is not the case, this doctrine can perhaps be preserved and made to serve a rational purpose once respondeat superior is understood as a device for the imposition of a non-fault liability for calculable harm. Upon this assumption, the entrepreneur should be liable only and always if he can calculate the harm likely to be caused by his enterprise and is thus in a poisition to insure against liability for such harm. If his contractor, too, is in such position, he should be jointly liable, while claims against him for indemnity could, unless stipulated, be limited to "moral" fault. True, this would leave the burden on the entrepreneur where the contractor is neither insured nor financially responsible. But this result is sound in that it will induce insurance of insurable loss. Occasional attempts to hold employers for the employment of financially irresponsible contractors would thus find a rational basis.[80]

While the doctrine of the independent contractor has been used to isolate the entrepreneur against liabilities

---

38 YALE L. J. 584, 720 (1929); Steffen, *Independent Contractor and the Good Life*, 2 U. of CHI. L. REV. 501 (1935); Harper, *The Basis of the Immunity of an Employer of an Independent Contractor*, 10 IND. L. J. 494 (1935). For an analysis of New York cases see N. Y. STATE LAW REVISION COMMISSION, REPORT (1939) 409-642, *Liability of Employer for the Negligence of an Independent Contractor*; and in general Note, 8 A. L. R. (2d) 267 (1949).

[79] Seavey, supra note 6, 456.

[80] See Lawrence v. Shipman, 39 Conn. 586, 590 (1873): "If a person having an interest in a job which naturally exposes others to peril, should attempt to shield himself from responsibility by contracting with a bankrupt mechanic, I think the employer might be subjected for damages done by the contractor. . . ." The plaintiff had claimed that the employment of a person financially irresponsible was equivalent to the employment of an incompetent person. It seems feasible that future courts on similar grounds will hold an employer for having employed an uninsured contractor.

which he could not be expected to calculate and insure against, the *"scope of employment"* doctrine has been used or abused to extend the entrepreneur's liability to all calculable harm without regard to technical qualifications of the servant's causative conduct as within or without his authority. The word "servant" has thus come to mean—in Professor Seavey's words—no more "than a person for whose physical acts under specified conditions the master is responsible"[81] and the doctrine has lost its usefulness as a test for the distribution of enterprise losses.

Since human beings are not machines the entrepreneur's liability can obviously not be limited to acts strictly within the necessary activities of the enterprise. On the other hand, equally obviously, not all conduct of every agent of the enterprise can be imputed to the entrepreneur. Courts have been inclined to deny the employer's liability for the servant's "frolic." Yet, since some harm from a normal number of frolics is part of the hazards of the enterprise, courts have been urged to bear in mind the risk-spreading justification of the doctrine of respondeat superior and to "reach conclusions which will further the policy upon which the justification rests."[82] The issue is not whether the servant intended to act within his employment,[83] but whether "in view of what the servant was actually employed to do, it was probable that he would do what he did"[84] or, in other words, whether his harmful conduct was typical for the enterprise in which he was employed.

Finally, and perhaps most significantly, under a rationalization of enterprise liability as of a liability for negligence without fault, the existence or availability of liability insurance could take its rightful place. That the harmful activity was insured or could have been insured, should be recognized rather than concealed as a decisive factor in the jury's

---

[81] Seavey, supra note 6, 465 n.49.

[82] Y. B. Smith, *Frolic and Detour*, 23 COL. L. REV. 444, 460 (1923). See also id. at 724.

[83] See Gleason v. Seaboard Air Line R. R., 278 U. S. 349, 49 Sup. Ct. 161 (1929); Y. B. Smith, supra note 82, 724.

[84] Y. B. Smith, supra note 82, 724.

finding of negligence without fault.[85] What is now referred to as the "prejudicial effect" on the jury of its knowledge of insurance would thus appear as a legitimate basis of its findings. And the apparent paradox of an immune entrepreneur forfeiting his immunity by taking out insurance could become an integral part of our tort law. Non-suable charities, infants, spouses, and parents[86] could be included in future general schemes of loss distribution.

§ 20.   b. *Owners and operators of automobiles.* In many countries the automobile owner is liable as such for the damage caused by his "enterprise."[87] While the French courts have reached this result by a rather artificial extension of the liability for inanimate things,[88] fault presumptions have been used in Argentina, Austria, Finland, and

---

[85] See Part I, note 156.

[86] See Part I, notes 153-155.

[87] See Société des Nations, *Institut International pour l'Unification du Droit Privé, Responsabilité Civile des Automobilistes, Étude Préliminaire,* 28 (1935); *Unification Internationale en Matière de Responsabilité Civile et d'Assurance Obligatoire des Automobilistes* 18, 19 (1940); JANNOTT, KRAFTFAHR-ZEUGHAFTPFLICHT—RECHT UND VERSICHERUNG IM IN- UND AUSLAND (1937); Deak, *Liability and Compensation for Automobile Accidents—A Survey of Foreign Legislation,* 21 MINN. L. REV. 123 (1937). Most laws hold the "owner" liable (Finland, Italy, Norway, Sweden). But others are satisfied with some measure of control. See the "Halter" in Germany, the "Betriebsunternehmer" in Austria, and the "detenteur" or "guardien" in France.

[88] Article 1384 (1) of the French Civil Code provides in part for the liability for harm caused by "those things one has in his custody." This article, though but a restatement of the Roman liability for things dangerously placed (e.g. on a window), was "discovered" for the purpose of rationalizing the liability of mechanical enterprise by the Belgian scholar Laurent [PRINCIPES DU DROIT CIVIL FRANÇAIS, t. XX, No. 639] and has since been applied for that purpose by the courts [See the celebrated decision of the Chambre Civile of June 11, 1896, S. 1897, 1.17]. This judicial legislation was recognized and confirmed by the Law of November 7, 1922 by an amendment of Article 1384 (1). For a full discussion and references to the abounding writings in this field, see 2 MAZEAUD, RESPONSABILITÉ CIVILE 2 et seq., 220 et seq. (4th ed., 1949). For South American law see e.g. ORGAZ, RESPONSA-BILIDAD POR EL HECHO DE LAS COSAS INANIMADAS (1931).

Italy, and express statutory provisions have been enacted elsewhere.[89]

In this country automobile liability followed the pattern of the railroads' liability for negligence.[90] As in the law of railroad liability the need for the substitution of the entre-preneur's liability for that of an often financially irrespon-sible actor has produced many artificial devices. In the field of automobile liability, however, the popular feeling that the owner is more likely to pay than the driver and that he who originates danger by setting a car upon the highway should be responsible,[91] has not, apart from statutes, pro-duced a general vicarious liability of the owner.[92] Only where the owner had in fact retained control over the operation of the car or where a presumption of such control is based on his presence in the car, has such liability been established.[93] While the admonitory policy underlying this limitation is obvious ("you shall watch your driver"), the related "family purpose doctrine"[94] is, it is submitted, an expression of a developing primarily compensatory trend. Under that doctrine the car owner is liable for harm caused

---

[89] See in general Maurice Picard, *Pour une loi sur la réparation des acci-dents d'automobiles*, REV. GEN. ASS. TERR. (1931) 613; Gorphe, *La responsabilité du fait des automobiles en droit comparé etc.*, REV. CRIT. LEGIS. ET JURIS. (1935) 150.

[90] See Part I, § 6.

[91] PROSSER, TORTS 499.

[92] Early attempts in that direction have remained isolated. In Sleath v. Wilson, 9 Carr & Payne 607, 173 Eng. Rep. 976 (1839) the owner of a carriage was held liable in a frolic case because "he had put it in the servant's power to mismanage the carriage." Florida seems to be the only jurisdiction in which a car owner is held generally liable for the negligent operation of his dangerous instrumentality. Southern Cotton Oil Co. v. Anderson, 80 Fla. 441, 86 So. 629 (1920); Lynch v. Walker, 159 Fla. 268, 31 So. (2d) 268 (1947).

[93] See Harper and Kime, *The Duty to Control the Conduct of Another*, 43 YALE L. J. 886, 888 et seq. (1934).

[94] See e.g. Lattin, *Vicarious Liability and Family Automobile*, 26 MICH. L. REV. 846 (1928). But cf. RESTATEMENT, AGENCY § 238 (1933), rejecting the doctrine. As to the possible extension of the doctrine to things other than automobiles, see Notes, 16 MINN. L. REV. 870 (1932); 6 SO. CAL. L. REV. 340 (1933).

by a member of his household in driving the car with his permission or acquiescence.[95] Rationalizations in terms of the current terminology must fail. Liability is neither based on fault nor on a master-servant relationship. The true rationale of the doctrine appears, I believe, in its limitation to harm done by a car operated for a "family purpose." Broad interpretations of this requirement as including driving for the driver's own pleasure, indicate that what is intended is the limitation of this liability for "negligence without fault" to harm typically caused in the owner's "business" as a householder.[96] This test should replace, under this doctrine as under similar statutory rules,[97] the common foreseeability test which has caused difficulties similar to those arising under the "scope of employment" rule of respondeat superior.[98] Only the extension of the owner's liability to unauthorized use might require legislation, though there are many indications for a return of the "dangerous instrument" doctrine.[99] Recognition of the owner's liability for negligence without fault would give the injured party the choice between a complaint claiming only, and limited to, damages for typical harm and one claiming damages for foreseeable harm based on the defendant's moral negligence committed by entrusting the car to an unfit person.

§ 21.   c. *"Immune" entrepreneurs.* (1) The limitation of *government* immunity[100] is still based on distinctions about

---

[95] See PROSSER, TORTS 500. The owner has even been held liable for an accident negligently caused by his minor son's guest. Cohen v. Whiteman, 75 Ga. App. 286, 43 S. E. (2d) 184 (1947).

[96] See PROSSER, TORTS 501.

[97] See PROSSER, TORTS 504.

[98] See supra § 19.

[99] See Horack, *The Dangerous Instrument Doctrine*, 26 YALE L. J. 224 (1916); Note, *Motor Cars as Dangerous Things, Opportunity of Inspection*, 3 MODERN L. REV. 235 (1940); Seavey, supra note 6, at 454; Patterson, *Required Motor Vehicle Insurance in New York*, 18 J. AM. INS. No. 8, pp. 13, 14 (1941). Regarding proposed legislation see SOCIÉTÉ DES NATIONS, op. cit. supra note 81, at 8, 30; UNIFICATION etc., op. cit. supra note 81, at 19, 31, 36.

[100] See supra § 16.

which little can be said "except that they exist, and that they are highly artificial."[101] It has come to be generally recognized that the usual criteria of "governmental," in contrast to "proprietary," activities do not coincide with the underlying economic test as to whether and when it is more appropriate to charge losses typically caused by a hazardous governmental activity to the beneficiaries of that activity or to the taxpayer.

Perhaps some clarity can be brought into what has been called "the most hopelessly confused subject of the law"[102] by approaching the thought originally underlying the immunity rule with the terminology here proposed. That "the King can do no wrong" is still true. There is no need and no way to admonish him by the threat of liability. But this rule does not preclude the King's compensatory liability for a "negligence" or "nuisance" which is not "really" a wrong but merely the basis, only historically explainable, for a liability for negligence without fault aimed at the distribution of calculable loss. Limitation of this liability to harm typically caused by the hazardous activity would permit both legislators and judges to deny immunity where full liability under the foreseeability test would place an inequitable burden on government funds or procure an unjustifiable windfall to the injured party.

Under this theory such activities as the supplying of water, gas, and electricity, the construction of highways or the operation of vehicles[103] would clearly subject the defendant municipality to liability for harm typically caused by such activities with or without the occurrence of a moral fault. This would apply to any activity which, being hazard-

---

[101] PROSSER, TORTS 1074.

[102] VAN DUSEN, MUNICIPALITIES AND THE LAW IN ACTION 173 (1943) with regard to a problem of labor law.

[103] See e.g. City Council of Augusta v. Lombard, 99 Ga. 282, 25 S. E. 772 (1896) (water); Brantman v. Canby, 119 Minn. 396, 138 N. W. 671 (1912) (gas); Poset v. North Birmingham, 154 Ala. 511, 45 So. 663 (1907) (electricity); Engelking v. Spokane, 59 Wash. 446, 110 Pac. 25 (1910) (highway); Knauth, *Government Liability for Aircraft Damage*, 37 ILL. L. REV. 359 (1943) (aircraft).

ous, would itself entail negligence liability were it not for its toleration and encouragement because of its preponderant social value. Where this factor is absent, as in many of the frequent cases involving recreational facilities,[104] the plaintiff would be without a remedy except possibly where he has paid a consideration.[105] Immunity even against liability for negligence without fault could be maintained without inconsistency for those activities which in a narrower sense may be called "governmental," such as the exercise of judicial or legislative discretion or the operation of a police force.[106]

Predicating governmental liability on the insurability of the harm caused would explain those seemingly anomalous decisions in which immunity was denied because of the existence of liability insurance.[107] The taking of such insurance would probably be facilitated by the exclusion from that liability of potentially unlimited claims for "foreseeable" harm.

(2) Similar considerations apply to the immunity of *charities* which, owing its origin to accident[108] and devoid of a valid rationalization,[109] has been recognized as untenable at this time when, in Justice Rutledge's words, "much of modern charity or philanthropy is 'big business' in its

---

[104] See e.g. Stuver v. Auburn, 171 Wash. 76, 17 P. (2d) 614 (1932) (merry-go-round); Royston v. Charlotte, 278 Mich. 255, 270 N. W. 288 (1936) (swing).

[105] See Rome v. L. & L. Indemn. Co., 181 La. 630, 160 So. 121 (1935); PROSSER, TORTS 1071.

[106] See e.g. Lamont v. Stavanaugh, 129 Minn. 321, 152 N. E. 720 (1915); Rhodes v. Kansas City, 167 Kan. 719, 208 P. (2d) 275 (1949); 6 McQUILLIN, THE LAW OF MUNICIPAL CORPORATIONS § 2802 (2d ed. 1937, Supp. 1947). The preservation of governmental immunity regarding those activities the continuation of which could be endangered by a false claim racket, would have to be left to legislation. The formula here proposed cannot solve this policy question any better than the present classification.

[107] See supra Part I, note 93.

[108] See President and Dir. of Georgetown College v. Hughes, 130 F. (2d) 810, at 815 (D. C. 1942) with historical references.

[109] See Part I, § 6.

field."[110] Indeed where liability insurance is available, the immunity rule cannot even be justified by the tenuous argument opposing the diversion of trust funds.[111] It can only be hoped that those still isolated decisions which deny immunity where such a fund is protected by insurance,[112] will soon be good law. This development could be promoted by limiting the tort liability of charitable enterprises to harm typically caused by hazardous activities.

(3) The related problem of the tort liability of *trusts* seems closer to a solution in the sense here proposed. Here as in the case of charity and government activities the plaintiff's limitation to a recovery against the immediate actor (public official, employee of charity, or trustee), has been found unsatisfactory where harm is caused by a hazardous enterprise activity. All too often the defendant proves financially irresponsible and a windfall would accrue to what has now often become a profit-making enterprise.

The first shift of the risk occurred when the trustee was given a right to indemnity against the trust estate in cases of strict liability.[113] A further step was the granting, in such cases, of a direct remedy to the injured against the estate,[114] coupled, more recently, with the limitation of the trustee's liability according to the scope of his recovery from the estate.[115]

Though the application of this rule to all cases of tort liability has been strongly advocated,[116] the injured suing in negligence is still limited to his remedy against the trustee. But a new and highly significant development is foreshadowed in Sections 13 and 14 of the Uniform Trusts Act,

---

[110] President and Dir. of Georgetown College v. Hughes, supra note 108, at 824.

[111] See Part I, § 6.

[112] See supra Part I, note 98.

[113] Bennett v. Wyndham, 4 De G. F. & J. 259, 45 Eng. Rep. 1183 (Ch. 1862).

[114] In re Raybould, 1 Ch. 199 (1900).

[115] Smith v. Rizzuto, 133 Neb. 655, 660, 276 N. W. 406, 409 (1937).

[116] Fulda and Pond, *Tort Liability of Trust Estates*, 41 COL. L. REV. 1332, 1356 (1941).

which so far has been adopted in Louisiana, Nevada, North Carolina, Oklahoma, and South Dakota. Under those provisions a person injured by any tort committed by the trustee in the administration of the trust may sue the estate (and the trustee if paying such claim may sue the estate for reimbursement), (1) if the tort was a "common incident" of the kind of business activity in which the trustee was properly engaged for the trust, and (2) in any other case in which neither he nor his officers or employees were "guilty of personal fault in incurring the liability."

It is submitted that the Uniform Trusts Act is the first statute in which the existence of two different types of liability within the common law rule of "negligence" is expressly recognized: (1) a liability for harm typically caused (as a "common incident") by an enterprise, shifted from the immediate actor to a profiting and calculating entrepreneur; (2) that individual's liability for "personal fault." Several corrections, however, seem necessary in the light of the theory here proposed.

It has been pointed out that the Act by giving the trustee a right to reimbursement even in cases of personal fault (where his tort was a common incident of the enterprise) has created a new injustice though removing one case of injustice from the law.[117] Moreover, absence of personal fault is made a sufficient basis of enterprise liability even if the trustee's tort was not a "common incident" of the enterprise. It is submitted that personal fault in this connection should be understood as that type of negligence of which— in the draftsman's words—"ordinary business men" are occasionally guilty "in the operation of any business;"[118] in other words, we should exclude cases of moral negligence from the operation of the rule besides limiting it to common incidents of the enterprise. The use of the term "personal fault" for negligence both with and without fault causes an unnecessary difficulty.

Another flaw in the wording of the statute is the inclusion

---

[117] Id. at 1350 et seq.
[118] 3 BOGERT, TRUSTS AND TRUSTEES § 734 (1946 perm. ed.).

in "personal fault" of a servant's tort. If the trustee-master's liability, notwithstanding fault language, is strict in nature, the trustee should be permitted to recover from the estate wherever he is held liable for his servant whether or not the latter committed a "personal fault."

Rephrased in terms of a consistent theory of negligence without fault, Sections 13 and 14 of the Uniform Trusts Act would permit the injured and the trustee to recover for harm calculably caused by that enterprise against the estate wherever the "tort" was committed as a "common incident"[119] of that enterprise and not caused by the trustee's moral fault. In jurisdictions which have not enacted these provisions, similar results could perhaps be reached under the common law.

§ 22.   d. *Manufacturers and distributors.* Difficult as it is to prove the "negligence" of any of the entrepreneurs previously discussed, such proof becomes virtually impossible where a member of the consuming public attempts to localize the cause of a harmful defect in a product of the multifarious and complex processes of modern mass manufacture and distribution. Is it preferable in such a case to allocate the loss to the consumer or to an entrepreneur who, though possibly "innocent," is a link in the chain of those entrepreneurs deriving profit from hazardous activities one of which has caused the harm? Is it preferable in such a case to allocate the loss to a consumer to whom it would be an incalculable catastrophe, or to an entrepreneur who can protect himself against just that kind of loss by insurance or price computation? To pose these questions is to answer them. In fact, both judges and juries have tended to protect the consumer by devices such as the virtual elimination of the "privity" requirement of contract law or of the foreseeability test of tort law.[120]

---

[119] See also Pound, *The End of Law as Developed in Legal Rules and Doctrines,* 27 HARV. L. REV. 195, 233 (1914), distinguishing damages "incident to the undertaking."

[120] See Part I, § 8.

But here, again, a re-formulation of the rules so adopted for purposes foreign to their origin seems imperative. The sound growth of the law is hampered when an automobile manufacturer can be held liable for harm typically caused by a defective wheel only upon a finding of the "presence of a known danger, attendant upon a known use;"[121] or when a can manufacturer's liability for harm atypically caused by a can-opener can be denied only because the harm could not "reasonably be foreseen and is not within the compass of reasonable probability."[122] Limitation of the manufacturer's liability there must be. But foreseeability, proximate causation, violation of duty, or privity are poor tests, completely foreign to economic reality. Nevertheless, the traditional language of negligence liability can perhaps be preserved by recognizing that this language in this field has come to express what has here been called a liability for negligence without fault for harm typically caused by the defendant's hazardous activity; a liability which, in Justice Traynor's words, is imposed because "the risk of injury can be insured against by the manufacturer and distributed among the public as a cost of doing business."[123]

The problem whether, and if so how, proof of causation by a particular defendant manufacturer or distributor can be dispensed with for the purpose of protecting the consumer, has perhaps been brought closer to a solution by a decision of the California Supreme Court. Two members of a hunting party were held jointly liable because it was clear that one of them had negligently shot the plaintiff.[124] There

---

[121] MacPherson v. Buick Motor Co., 217 N. Y. 382, 111 N. E. 1050 (1916).

[122] Boyd v. American Can Co., 249 App. Div. 644, 292 N. Y. Supp. 689 (1936).

[123] Escola v. Coca-Cola Bottling Co., 24 Cal. (2d) 453, 462, 150 P. (2d) 436, 441 (1944). See also Justice Traynor's concurring opinion in Gordon v. Aztec Brewing Co., 33 Cal. (2d) 514, 523, 203 P. (2d) 522, 528 (1949). But cf. Pound, *Law in the Service State: Freedom versus Equality*, 36 A. B. A. J. 977, 981 (1950).

[124] Summers v. Tice, 33 Cal. (2d) 80, 199 P. (2d) 1 (1948). See supra Part I, notes 124, 125.

is no reason why the rationale of that decision, which shifts to the defendant the burden of proof in the case of alternative causation by a dangerous activity, should not be borrowed in the law of enterprise liability for allocating harm caused by a defect arising at an unidentified place in the processes of mass production and mass distribution.[125] True, neither hunter would have been held by the California court had he not been proved negligent in having fired a shot in the plaintiff's direction. But even without the identification and proof of such a negligent act, the rationale of this case would be applicable to the products liability of manufacturers and large distributors whose liability is recognized to be based on negligence without fault. False-claim rackets could still be discouraged by adopting or maintaining strict requirements as to the proof of harm caused.

Another problem concerns the ultimate allocation of risks between the retailer and the manufacturer. The choice seems clear where, as in the case of branded canned goods, the manufacturer takes credit for his product and can protect its integrity. There is little justification for holding the retailer in the absence of moral negligence where he "has no superior means of knowing the contents of the can than the purchaser."[126] A statutory strict liability of the "brand-

---

[125] Similar considerations may underlie that rule of pleading under which plaintiffs have been permitted to sue two entrepreneur defendants in the alternative if being in doubt as to which is liable. See S. & C. Clothing Co. v. U. S. Trucking Corp., 216 App. Div. 482, 215 N. Y. Supp. 349 (1926) (merchandise lost by either trucking or warehouse company). See also Kraft v. Smith, 24 Cal. (2d) 124, 74 P. (2d) 528 (1944) (either of two physicians negligent); and in general CLARK, CODE PLEADING 393 (2d ed. 1947).

[126] Julian v. Lauenberger, 16 Misc. 646, 38 N. Y. Supp. 1052 (1896). See also MELICK, THE SALE OF FOOD AND DRINK 23 et seq. (1936); *Products Liability*, Part I, note 1. See also the controversies between Waite [34 MICH. L. REV. 494 (1936); 23 MINN. L. REV. 612 (1939)] and Brown [23 MINN. L. REV. 585 (1939)]; and between Eldredge [89 U. of PA. L. REV. 306 (1941); 45 DICK. L. REV. 269 (1941)] and Farage [45 DICK. L. REV. 159, 282 (1941)]. But cf. 1 WILLISTON, THE LAW GOVERNING SALES OF GOODS AT COMMON LAW § 242 (1924).

ing seller" would work as a "lightning rod" for the retailer who would thus be relieved, without further statutory interference, of a liability which has often been criticized with much justification.[127] It seems regrettable that this solution, proposed in the First Draft of a Revised Uniform Sales Act, has apparently been abandoned.[128]

Even where a direct remedy is available against the producer, there should perhaps be an additional liability of those distributors who, "for purposes of insurance, absorption and reduction of loss [are] . . . in a position closely akin to manufacturers."[129] Indeed such distributors may in many cases, as where they distribute the products of several smaller producers, be more capable of calculating and distributing the risk than the producers themselves. Perhaps this failure to segregate those situations accounts for the general preservation of the liability of distributors. A nonlegislative distinction between "large distributors" and retailers within common law rules seems all the more desirable as no constitutional way has yet been found to draw such a distinction by statute.[130] Juries could probably be relied upon to exempt from liability for negligence without fault small distributors unable to calculate, and insure against, losses caused by their merchandise.

---

[127] See Report and Second Draft, REVISED UNIFORM SALES ACT 24 (1941); Waite, *Retail Responsibility and Judicial Law Making*, 34 MICH. L. REV. 494 (1936).

[128] Compare the mimeographed First Draft (1940) with the Report and Second Draft of the REVISED UNIFORM SALES ACT (1941); and in general, *Products Liability*, Part I, note 1, at § 38.

[129] Report and Second Draft, REVISED UNIFORM SALES ACT 124 (1941).

[130] Id. at 116. The proposed liability scheme would necessitate the broadening of the retailer's insurance protection [see LANGE, ADDRESS, Convention of National Retail Dry Goods Association (1939) 2, 10], and the substitution of direct coverage for the present coverage by "certificates" on the producer's policy. [See Perryman in CAHILL, PRODUCTS LIABILITY INSURANCE, 21 Proceedings Cas. Act. Sec., Nos. 43, 44 (1935)].

§ 23.   4. FAULT AND NON-FAULT NEGLIGENCE IN THE
         LAWS OF TORTS AND CRIMES

The present negligence language of the courts must serve
both the primarily compensatory function of enterprise liability and the primarily admonitory function of the original
liability for fault. This fact has not only been detrimental
to the development of enterprise liability but has equally
affected those other types of negligence liability which, implying blame, may appropriately be called liabilities for
"moral" negligence.[131]

The distinction here proposed can, I believe, aid in the
clarification of both types of liability.[132] But "moral" negligence and negligence without fault do not occupy the whole
field of what is now referred to as "negligence." There remains the liability for "objective" negligence not connected
with the hazards of modern enterprise, which seems to defy
classification. For, on the one hand, that objective negligence can hardly be called "moral," since it is determined
by a fictitious foreseeability test similar to that of negligence
without fault and strict liability.[133] On the other hand, objective negligence, with its strong undercurrent of censure
in language and ideology,[134] cannot wholly be segregated

---

[131] See Part I, §§ 10, 11. Shortcomings of the related "wilful and
wanton misconduct" terminology are ably discussed by Burrell, *A New
Approach to the Problem of Wilful and Wanton Misconduct*, [1949] INS. L. J.
716 (1949).

[132] See Bohlen, *Old Phrases and New Facts*, 83 U. of PA. L. REV. 305,
312 (1935): "There is no reason . . . why the same rules should apply
where the responsibility is based, in theory at least, and still too largely
also in fact, on the wrongdoing of the defendant and where, as in workmen's compensation cases and insurance cases, culpability, real or legal-
istically assumed, has no part in determining the existence or extent of
responsibility." This prophetic "dictum" is followed by the exhortation
directed to the courts to explain openly the "real reasons for their decisions."

[133] See supra §§ 13-16.

[134] This undercurrent is apparent in the usual formulation of the
objective negligence rule in terms of "one must . . ." [see e.g., HOLMES,

from "moral" negligence. The existence of this twilight zone should, however, not prevent us from a separation of the clearly separable fields of enterprise liability for negligence without fault and non-enterprise liability for "moral" negligence.

The doctrine of res ipsa loquitur, which originally facilitated proof of fault, has been forced into an "unhappy marriage" with the presumption of negligence without fault in carriers' liability.[135] Once the "negligence" liability of modern enterprise has been rerationalized as a liability for negligence without fault for calculable harm, res ipsa can be relieved of the danger of being compelled to find fault where none can be found[136] and returned to its original meaning of a rule of evidence. And respondeat superior, once it is no longer needed to create a non-fault liability in fault language, could develop a policy justifying that language by a return to the selection and control idea of its early stages.[137]

Once moral negligence is no longer the basis of the distribution of risks innocently incurred and can again be defined as blameworthy conduct, it may again become usable in criminal law which should punish only the conscious creation of risk.[138] Whether or not criminal negligence should be identified with, or even related to, tort negligence, is beyond the scope of this study.[139] But that relation

---

THE COMMON LAW 108 (1881)] or in the exceptional treatment of super- or sub-normal injurers who, under a consistent "objective" theory, would not be judged according to their superior or inferior knowledge or ability. But see Seavey, *Negligence—Subjective or Objective*, 41 HARV. L. REV. 1 (1927); RESTATEMENT, TORTS §§ 283, 289 Comment (n) (1934); Edgerton, supra note 57, 857.

[135] See Part I, § 5.
[136] See Part I, notes 30, 127.
[137] See Part I, § 3.
[138] See Wechsler-Michael, *A Rationale of the Law of Homicide*, 37 COL. L. REV. 701, 721 (1937).
[139] See Kirchheimer, *Criminal Omissions*, 55 HARV. L. REV. 615 (1942); HALL, PRINCIPLES OF CRIMINAL LAW 215 (1947); PROSSER, TORTS 10 et seq.; Hitschler, *Crimes and Civil Injuries*, 39 DICK. L. REV. 23 (1934). Regarding the related problem of the pre-

exists and has resulted in a hardly desirable intrusion into criminal law of the trend in tort law to base a compensatory liability on fault language.[140] In order to hold a railroad liable in tort for the death caused by a switchman who had misread a time table, or to hold a construction corporation for the death caused by a laborer who used too much powder in a blasting operation,[141] a jury would have to find negligence in inadvertence. That employees have in such cases occasionally been convicted of manslaughter may be attributable to the similar tour de force in the development of enterprise liability. Once civil law sanctions for the causation of calculable harm protect the injured without regard to the defendant's responsibility for the foreseeability of that harm, punishment adequate to the moral fault committed, that is, to that foreseeability, can become the rule in criminal law.[142]

To sum up: The negligence rule, though phrased in terms of fault, has, with regard to tort liabilities for dangerous enterprise, come to exercise a function of loss distribution previously developed mainly within rules of strict liability. This new function of "fault" liability has transformed its

---

judiciality in tort proceedings of criminal convictions see e. g. Note, *Criminal Judgments as Res Adjudicata in Civil Actions for Penalties*, 11 COL. L. REV. 170 (1911); NEW YORK LAW REVISION COMMISSION, Report (1939) 391 et seq.; Von Moschzisker, *Res Judicata*, 38 YALE L. J. 299, 325 (1929); SCHMIDT, FAUTE CIVILE ET FAUTE PÉNALE (1928) 71 et seq., 125 et seq.

[140] No opinion is expressed as to whether the present trend towards objectivation in the criminal law itself has been promoted by parallel trends in the law of torts. See Sayre, *The Present Significance of Mens Rea in the Criminal Law*, HARVARD LEGAL ESSAYS 399 (1934). Holmes, J., in Commonwealth v. Pierce, 138 Mass. 165, 52 Am. Rep. 264 (1884) expressly invokes the law of torts for justifying the promotion of external standards in the law of crimes "in the interest of the safety of all." Regarding legislative and judicial attempts at introducing "Criminal Liability of a Business Man for Conduct of his Employees," see Note, 38 J. CRIM. LAW AND CRIMINOLOGY 132 (1947).

[141] Regina v. Benge, 4 F. & F. 504, 176 Eng. Rep. 665 (1865); People v. Clemente, 146 App. Div. 109, 130 N. Y. Supp. 612 (1911).

[142] See Note, 31 CALIF. L. REV. 215 (1943).

central concepts of reprehensible conduct and "foreseeability" of harm in a way foreign to its language and original rationale and has thus produced in our present "negligence" language a series of misleading equivocations.

While neither statutory nor judicial legislation can or should attempt a wholesale reform of the well-established system of negligence liability, I believe that either statutory or judicial interpretation should recognize and resolve these equivocations, which hamper the natural growth of judicial as well as statutory law by concealing essential distinctions between the original field of negligence liability and the liability for "negligence without fault" of modern enterprise. Such recognition would, among other things, facilitate intelligent and intelligible instructions to the jury by limiting the present "foreseeability" test to harm caused by reprehensible conduct and by substituting for that test one of typicality with regard to harm caused by the lawful activities of hazardous enterprise.

Whether a man carelessly shooting at birds in a village street is to be held for injuries inflicted upon a bystander by a falling bird, should be determined according to whether a reasonable man in the defendant's place could have foreseen such injuries. But whether a railroad company is to be held for the drowning of four children chasing a kite across a frozen pond formed by the inadvertence of a railroad employee,[143] should be determined according to whether such result was typical for the hazards of the operation of a railroad and thus reasonably insurable. True, doubts will remain and this theory will not, any more than any other theory, resolve all problems. But one merit the author feels he can claim for his formulation of the negligence rule as applied to enterprise liability: juries and judges would no longer be misled by "horse and buggy rules in an age of machinery."[144]

---

[143] See Part I, § 1.
[144] James, *Accident Liability Reconsidered: The Impact of Liability Insurance,* 57 YALE L. J. 549, 569 (1948).

TABLE OF CASES

INDEX

www.ingramcontent.com/pod-product-compliance
Lightning Source LLC
Chambersburg PA
CBHW021944220326
41599CB00013BA/1678